# HOW TO AVOID
# PROBATE
## BY CREATING
## A LIVING TRUST

# HOW TO AVOID
# PROBATE
## BY CREATING
## A LIVING TRUST

### A Simple Yet Complete Guide

# GORDON MEAD BENNETT

*Founder of the National Center for
the Avoidance of Probate*

BARNES
&NOBLE
BOOKS
NEW YORK

**A Barnes & Noble Publishing Book**

Copyright 2004 © by Gordon Mead Bennett

Library of Congress Cataloging-in-Publication Data

Bennett, Gordon Mead.
  How to avoid probate by creating a living trust: a simple yet complete guide / Gordon Mead Bennett.
     p. cm.
  Includes index.
  ISBN 0-7607-5472-1
  1. Living trusts—United States—Popular works. 2. Probate law and practice—United States—Popular works. 3. Estate planning—United States—Popular works. I. Title.
KF734.Z9B46 2004
346.7305'2—dc22

                                        2003021843


Designer: Joseph Rutt
Illustration: Sandy Nichols
Cover Design: Christine Heun


Printed and bound in the United States of America

1 3 5 7 9 10 8 6 4 2

First Edition

This book is an overview of basic legal concepts, not a substitute for a lawyer or an answer to every possible legal question. The laws touched upon in this book vary considerably from jurisdiction to jurisdiction and change frequently. Be sure to consult a lawyer knowledgeable about the current laws in your state or jurisdiction if you have a particular legal problem. Note that names and addresses used on sample forms, and in examples cited throughout the text, are hypotheticals created to illustrate particular points rather than depictions of actual scenarios involving real people; any resemblance to actual persons is unintentional.

While Barnes & Noble Publishing and the author have used best efforts in writing this book, they make no representations or warranties as to its accuracy and completeness. They also do not make any implied warranties of merchantability or fitness for a particular purpose. Any advice given in this book is not guaranteed or warranted and it may not be suitable for every factual situation. Neither Barnes & Noble Publishing nor the author shall be liable for any losses suffered by any reader of this book. Barnes & Noble Publishing neither endorses nor has any affiliation with the National Center for the Avoidance of Probate. Should the reader contact the National Center for the Avoidance of Probate for independent advice, Barnes & Noble Publishing shall have no liability associated therewith.

The quotes in this book have been drawn from many sources, and are assumed to be accurate as quoted in their previously published forms. Although every effort has been made to verify the quotes and sources, the publisher cannot guarantee their perfect accuracy.

*To my devoted and beautiful Laura who stood by
my side for fifty-four years—yet still found time to
feed her mind by reading three books a week.
I hope this one pleases you, my dear.*

# Contents

## Introduction

# Behind the Legal Curtain

I am not an attorney. I am an author. In fact, I spent forty years of my life in the ownership and management of motion picture theaters, a vocation completely unrelated to estate planning. How does having seen more than four thousand movies in a lifetime qualify me as an expert on living trusts?

It doesn't!

The fact is that anyone could have written this book. You could have written it. Your next-door neighbor could have written it. Living trusts are regulated and made utilitarian and safe for public consumption by the very fiduciary laws that have protected the savings and investments of the public for centuries. All that is needed is curiosity and the common sense to apply those laws to a different technique of ownership called a trust.

And it helps to have had your family scalded by the legal profession once or twice, as has happened to me.

*Scalding Number One:* My father died in 1974. My mother's death followed in 1988. Our parents had told my brother, sister, and me that upon their deaths, their estate would flow to us in just a few days at little or no legal cost. Ah, peace of mind. There was nothing for us to bother with or learn, and I could get back to the business of watching movies and other self-indulgences. Ignorance is bliss.

Upon the death of my mother (the surviving spouse), it took the attorney fourteen months and fourteen thousand dollars in legal costs to transfer what was left of my parents' estate to their kids.

Years later I learned that the attorney (who professed to be a close friend of my father) had intentionally placed the estate in something called a testamentary trust rather than a living trust without explaining the difference to my parents. A testamentary trust not only requires all the trappings and expenses of probate at death, but because the attorney has prepared all the paperwork of a trust while still getting to probate the estate, it also doubles the attorney's fee.

*Scalding Number Two:* The estate of my father's older and childless sister approximated $1million. She hated her deceased husband's relatives and chose to write a new will disinheriting them and leaving everything to three nephews and two nieces on her side of the family. Having learned from experience, I approached a stockbroker friend of mine for help.

"The woman has estate tax problems, capital gains tax problems, probate problems, and an excellent chance of a will contest by her disgruntled in-laws," explained the broker. "What she needs is a living trust."

A living trust? I had no idea what a living trust was. And so it seemed like a good time to start asking some questions. To keep my aunt's estate out of trouble and selfishly protect my own inheritance, I spent the next three years reading and studying everything I could get my hands on in regard to estate planning and living trusts.

But alas, ninety-five-year-old childless aunts are pretty much set in their ways. Armed with fresh information after reading yet another living trust book, I would enthusiastically approach her each week with a new set of reasons why she should commit her affairs to a living trust. But after each of my sales pitches I would always be met with a polite but curt "No."

This went on for years as she shunned my good intentions (and a living trust), putting her entire faith instead in the nice little boy next door who had faithfully mowed her lawn and shoveled her walk before becoming her attorney years later.

Though the family averted a will contest at her death, the nice little boy next door eventually billed the estate for just under $30,000 to probate my aunt's large but relatively simple estate. The job could have been handled very nicely with a $400–$500 living trust.

## THE NATIONAL CENTER FOR THE AVOIDANCE OF PROBATE

My three years of reading books on living trusts and listening to my aunt's pithy refusals to invest in such a program were not wasted, however. Retiring from the movies, I founded the National Center for the Avoidance of Probate (NCAP), where I could share the estate-planning knowledge that I had gained through reading hundreds of books on the subject, and perhaps prevent others from also being scalded. It seemed to me that it would be nice if everyone in America knew some of the basics of estate planning—such as the fact that a will does not avoid probate, or that joint ownership of assets with children subjects the parents to their children's legal problems with creditors as well as exposes the children to huge capital gains taxes.

However, I was met with the rage of many attorneys and a Michigan Bar Association that claimed that to dispense such information was practicing law without a license. They claimed that only an attorney was free to pass such information on to the public. I countered that if this were true, the legal profession had been doing a pretty rotten job of it. Most of the few citizens that had a will were falsely convinced that they would avoid probate, and millions of parents had committed the blunder of including their children on the titles and deeds of their assets. Instead of showing clients how to reduce estate-planning time and costs, the legal profession seemed to be intentionally exploiting the ignorance of the public for the purpose of racking up what most experts believe to be roughly $15 billion annually in unnecessary legal fees.

Thirteen years have now passed and my original three-year investment of time in living trust knowledge has multiplied many times. The

National Center for the Avoidance of Probate responds to the combined e-mail and telephone calls of a hundred people or more daily from across the United States, attempting to clear up confusion regarding estate planning, wills, trusts, joint ownership, and estate taxes and helping them develop their own living trusts sans attorney. The NCAP's Web site is visited by an average of 15,000 Americans every month, and over the years, the NCAP has become a lightning rod for thousands of authenticated cases of attorney malpractice and malfeasance in the field of estate planning.

## NORMAN DACEY'S *HOW TO AVOID PROBATE*

To the dismay of the attorneys, a best-selling book, *How to Avoid Probate,* published in the early 1960s by estate planner Norman Dacey, blew the lid off the probate rip-off. Consequently, to stave off the public's interest in living trusts and preserve the legal fees plucked from the pockets of the public through the probate process, attorneys desperately sought to discredit him. In Dacey's opening chapter, he explains the almost impossible legal injunctions and spooking of his seminars by a New England Bar Association intent on destroying his credibility and preventing the truth from reaching the citizens of the Northeast. However, in the end, the protests and tricks of the New England Bar Association and others succeeded only in turning Dacey's book into a national best-seller and initiated the replacement of legal skullduggery with truth.

Dacey's book has now been out of print for a number of years. Why has the time come to revisit the subject of avoiding probate? Recently, the strategy to squash or disarm those that would blow the whistle on the attorneys has mutated. Faced for years with the argument that their "practicing law without a license" accusations infringed on the First Amendment rights of the non-attorneys who wrote books and lectured on the subject, the legal profession has apparently switched gears. The tactic now seems to be to enlist the help of and gain credibility from fellow attorneys employed at the state attorney general's office in boldly proclaiming that such non-attorneys are con men and scammers out to swindle away the savings of senior citizens. Hundreds of articles concerning the "traps" of non-attorneys appear monthly in the nation's daily and weekly newspapers and on the Internet; most writings of which have been okayed by unenlightened editors and webmasters who have taken the word of a fee-hungry legal profession. However, one of the hundreds of eye-opening facts you will learn from this book is the verity that all living trusts are legal—*there is no such thing as an illegal living trust.* Thus, the only possible scam in which you can become involved is in paying too much for your trust. As it turns out, attorneys generally charge more for a living trust than does anyone else, so they become the biggest scammers of them all!

Consequently, the purpose of this book is twofold. First, it discloses the misrepresentations, malpractice, and propaganda many attorneys, sympathizing bar associations, and state attorney general's offices are willing to speak, commit, and publish to maintain income from the lucrative cash cow of asset transfer to the next generation.

Second, because the lion's share of probate costs (sixty-five to seventy-five percent) goes to the attorney, estate planning is as much about avoiding attorneys at death as it is about avoiding probate. Therefore, this book reveals in easy-to-understand, layman's language how quickly and inexpensively almost anyone can privately establish a legal, foolproof, probate-avoiding, tax-saving living trust in just forty-eight to seventy-two hours—all without the assistance of a lawyer.

## THE "WIZARD" REVEALED

Now let's get back to the movies. After four decades of watching movies, I am often asked by friends and acquaintances just which is my all-time favorite scene. Most expect my reply to be the burning of Atlanta, the parting of the Red Sea, perhaps the perilous climb up the cliffs at Normandy Beach, or the efforts of some other Hollywood special effects genius.

None of the above. The most meaningful scene I have ever witnessed was from Victor Fleming's screen adaptation of author L. Frank

Baum's *The Wizard of Oz*. Since its first showing in 1939, hundreds of millions have witnessed Dorothy and her friends from the Yellow Brick Road cowering in front of the mighty wizard as he huffed, puffed, shouted, and terrorized his innocent and ignorant visitors.

And then the little dog Toto pulled away the curtain. Behind the folds of the drape was a frightened and bewildered old man frantically manipulating all kinds of wheels and levers in an effort to intimidate all those who came before him.

What a lesson Toto teaches us about the value of educating ourselves. When we allow professional wizards to exploit our ignorance, superstitions, fear, and propensity to believe only what we want to believe, we quickly become slaves to such tyrants. Nowhere is this lesson more apparent than in the field of estate planning. Nowhere is ignorance, superstition, and fear so costly and damning as in the arranging of an orderly transfer of our assets to our loved ones.

Just behind the legal curtain is a profession orchestrating hundreds of myths, fables, falsehoods, and shouts of "you will get in terrible trouble if you don't do as I say"—all of it designed to maintain a centuries-old stranglehold on the lucrative game of transferring assets to the next generation.

Allow me to transport you through a hidden portal into the backroom of estate planning and expose you to the truth—and savings of thousands of dollars in court costs, attorney fees, estate taxes, and frustrating months of delay. To begin your journey, simply read ahead.

# 1

# Why Your Will Is Worthless

**M**illions of Americans possess a Last Will and Testament that they paid an attorney several hundred dollars to draw. There is nothing wrong with that in itself. The problem is that most of those Americans have a false notion of what this document can do for them. The attorney most likely left them with the impression that their Last Will and Testament would avoid the long and expensive probate procedure at death. Indeed, the fact that they thought a will would avoid probate is the primary reason they purchased a will. Now, believing that all of their estate-planning needs have been cared for, they refuse to listen to the facts or investigate other possibilities.

The truth is that your Last Will and Testament will not avoid probate. For confirmation of this fact, take the will down to your bank tomorrow morning and ask the banker if the bank will release your savings accounts and other bank assets to your heirs after you die on the strength of what is written in the will. I promise you the answer will be a resounding "no."

Another test would be simply to put down this book right now, telephone the attorney that drew the will for you and ask point blank: "Will the will you have drawn for me avoid probate?"

This in-your-face challenge will place the attorney in a most uncomfortable bind. If he chooses to answer "yes," the attorney commits the malpractice of lying. His oath as an officer of the court forbids lying to

a client, and the attorney thus risks career-ending disbarment. Yet, if he chooses to speak the truth by saying "no," the attorney admits that since the day he drew your will, he has intentionally misled you, which destroys your confidence in him to represent you in the future.

But attorneys are noted for fast-thinking glibness. Your attorney will likely answer neither yes nor no! Instead, the attorney will put on his best courtroom face, lower his voice a full octave, and say something like this:

"Well, all wills are *subject* to probate."

Subject to? That's like saying if you jump off a bridge, you're subject to getting wet. You can bet the rent money on it! Nonetheless, that is about as close to the truth as an attorney will get in the matter of a Last Will and Testament avoiding probate.

So, if an attorney is under oath to tell his clients the truth, why didn't your attorney tell you that your will would not avoid probate at the time he sold it to you? The answer is simple: you didn't ask! Instead, you assumed it would avoid probate. You see, attorneys don't lie in fact; they lie by omission. Nowhere does it say that an attorney is obligated to tell you all of the facts. Hence, most attorneys refrain from disclosing any detail that would tend to reduce their present and future fees. If confronted later, the attorney can always fall back on double-speak and confusing legalese to defend his actions.

# INTESTATE VS. TESTATE PROBATE

There are also many mind games played in legal offices across America every day to involve the client's estate in the profitable process of probate. What follows is one of the very best. There are two kinds of probate at death:

- An *intestate* probate indicates that the decedent had no legal will at the time of death. In such intestate probate procedures, the court, through a court-appointed executor, must beat the bushes to locate the assets and then distribute the assets to the heirs according to rigid, ironclad laws of the state. The verbal wishes of the decedent while still alive carry absolutely no weight.

- A *testate* probate indicates that at death the decedent had a legal will. Should there be no successful challenges to that will by unnamed heirs or creditors, the assets usually are then distributed according to the bequests made by the decedent in the will. (See the chart on page 32 for a further comparison of testate and intestate probate.)

Of greatest importance here is to understand that either way, intestate or testate, *the decedent's estate must pass through months of agonizing and expensive probate.*

Most attorneys lecture their clients on the fact that they need a will to avoid their estate ending up in an intestate probate procedure. This, of course, is entirely true.

However, unbeknownst to the client, the attorney too often "accidentally" omits the word *intestate* from the explanation. Thus, the attorney warns his client:

"You must have a will to avoid a probate procedure."

This puts an entirely different spin on the attorney's narrative and is usually interpreted by the client to mean that if a person has no will, probate court will determine who gets the assets, and if the client has a will her estate will avoid probate! Because the client wants the right to determine who inherits her lifelong savings and real estate rather than forfeit that right to the state, the client jumps at the attorney's "you-must-have-a-will" bait which adds one more trout to the attorney's creel. The attorney is now in a position to skim thousands of dollars off the top of the client's estate in probate court at death and the client goes to her final rest innocently believing her estate will avoid probate.

If the heirs, under the impression that the parent's will was drawn to avoid probate, challenge the attorney, the attorney need only say that the deceased client, now unavailable to tell her side of the story, had incorrectly interpreted the attorney's words. She sure did! I do not believe any sane person would choose to draw a will knowing that such an effort would surely land her estate in exasperating and costly probate court!

---

### The Plain Truth

It is imperative to remember that either way, with or without a will, without a living trust your estate is headed for probate court, your heirs are about to be mugged out of what they rightfully had coming to them, and you've been had.

---

## THE HIGH COSTS OF PROBATE

Probate at death is a validating process that guarantees the authenticity and legality of your Last Will and Testament. At your death it permits your financial custodians (banks, credit unions, stockbrokers, or registrar of deeds) to safely release your savings accounts, stocks, real estate, and so forth, into the possession of your legal heirs, free from the fear of possible lawsuits by disinherited or disgruntled heirs.

The probate process takes twelve to twenty-four months, depending on the state in which you live (each state has its own maximum time limits for potential heirs and creditors to make their cases). The cost is a bit more difficult to get a handle on and ranges from three percent of the estate at the low end to fifteen percent at the high end, according to respected but differing sources such as *The Wall Street Journal,* the

American Association of Retired Persons (AARP), and the Estate Research Council. The legal profession naturally states a lower range of three to six percent enabling probate-advocating attorneys to put the best face possible on the probate procedure.

In addition to the attorney's fee (usually sixty-five to seventy-five percent of the total probate expense), the court costs include such items as court filing fees, appraisers, newspaper ads, stenographers, a personal representative's fee, a personal performance bond for the personal representative, the cost of the court's presence at safety deposit box openings, telephone calls, postage stamps, and the like. Until the probate process is completed and all costs settled, your bank and other financial custodians will simply refuse to release your bank assets, stocks, mutual funds, real estate, and other assets to your heirs.

Once probate court has determined that the will is indeed the last will you wrote, the court must 1) collect the funds owed to you by your debtors, 2) see to it that your creditors are paid, and 3) determine if the assets you claimed to own are indeed truly owned by you. These three essentials must all transpire and the attorneys, the undertaker, and the tax collector must be paid before the heirs of the estate can receive one dime of their inheritances.

During the course of the procedure the assets are usually frozen and left to twist and turn in the ups and downs of fluctuating markets. Most family financial needs must be put on hold (often for months) while the court is sifting through potential heirs, creditors, debtors, and possible legal challenges to the will.

Consequently, families of the recently deceased have for centuries been held hostage to probate attorneys who can take as long as they want and charge what they please. This locked-in, monopolistic financial bonanza for attorneys produces up to twenty percent of the general-practice attorney's annual income.

## WHO INVENTED PROBATE?

The probate system can be traced back more than twelve centuries. In the days of the Roman Empire, most of the citizens believed the world was flat and tended to be a mite superstitious. They were susceptible to just about any tale or legal maneuver the privileged and educated few could dream up. One of the best was a plan to levy a heavy surcharge on the families of the recently deceased by requiring that the written wishes of those that had died be proven or certified in a court of law. The court was called probate, which in Latin means, "to prove the will." All of the decedent's obligations to creditors and the government had to be satisfied before titled assets could pass from the decedent to the heirs. And of course, the attorneys were rewarded with a handsome fee to provide this service.

On the surface, probate was a noble idea. It was the first attempt of a civilized society to protect creditor from heir (and vice versa) and systematically pass the assets of the deceased on to the next generations. Like the spinning wheel and butter churn, this system served an immobile and unsophisticated society well for more than a millennium. It also became one of the most profitable wares on the lawyer's shelf. The family of the decedent, often gasping for usable funds, could wait for months—sometimes years—while their attorney took as long as he wanted and charged whatever he deemed fair to settle the decedent's often simple estate.

Today lifestyles are a far cry from what they were even a few generations ago. In the first few decades of the twentieth century, with the shortage of automobiles, electricity, and telephones, it often took months to first locate and then communicate with the relatives of a decedent. Since then, however, the advances in contemporary jet travel, satellites, computers, and the Internet have made it possible for people to be in almost instant communication with each other from nearly any spot on the globe. Thus, decisions of business, government, and finance must often be made in a matter of minutes. In contrast, the prolonged and torpid probate procedure that can financially and psychologically hold an entire family captive for months or even years has become outmoded and obsolete.

In 1969, the Uniform Probate Code, a combined effort of the American Bar Association and the National Conference of Commissioners on Uniform State Laws, was introduced and eventually adapted in whole or in part by eighteen states. The code was a voluntary plan to bring

*In law, nothing is certain but the expense.*

—SAMUEL BUTLER

consistency to the nation's maze of probate rules, regulations, customs, and attorney fees. Unfortunately, it took years of compromise to create a code to which the majority of lawyers could agree, and as a result, the watered-down Uniform Probate Code issued by the state legislatures was little more than a whitewashing of the old systems. This new code has generally been met with the disdain of lawyers who wish to continue to apply their individual sleight-of-hand tactics to the imperfect science of probate and charge whatever the traffic will bear.

This rejection by attorneys of the Uniform Probate Code has done little more than expose the American Bar Association's lack of power to enact any real reform when it comes to probate. In Great Britain, through a rearrangement of the courts, probate now rarely takes more than four or five weeks. However, in America, the no-financial-holds-barred, free enterprise champion of the world, where everyone is working an angle, probate remains a horse-and-buggy technique that unless updated and streamlined will inevitably invite revolt by the entire American electorate.

# WHY DO ATTORNEYS MISREPRESENT ESTATE PLANNING?

The many rumors that circulate regarding today's probate procedure are actually perpetuated by the legal profession's reluctance to set the record straight. The propagation of many worthless home remedies for avoiding probate (such as joint tenancy, to be discussed later), which could easily be dispelled with some professionalism by the attorneys, serves to lull the public into a state of false security that its estates are properly taken care of.

At death, however, reality sets in. The heirs are unceremoniously jerked back into the world of reality to find themselves sitting by helplessly for twelve to twenty-four months and watching three to fifteen percent of their inheritances detoured into the pockets of an attorney and the cash box of an archaic court system.

Why this subterfuge? Why this unwillingness to disclose all estate-planning facts to clients?

Of all the services performed by general-practice attorneys—such as divorce, property transfer, custody battles, bankruptcy, personal injury, dog bites, drunk driving, debt collection, and so forth—the transfer of assets to the next generation via the probate process now ranks second among all legal services (about ten percent below tax work) in the gleaning of legal fees from the public. It is a plain, hard fact that too many attorneys are interested in legal fees first and justice second.

In the lucrative probate process, the attorney's fee is calculated on the gross estate. As an example: a $1 million gross estate owes $700,000 in mortgages and other obligations. However, the percentage used to compute the attorney's legal fee will be reckoned against the $1 million gross estate rather than the net $300,000 the estate is actually worth.

As a general rule, the smaller the value of the estate, the greater the percentage of it will go for court costs and attorney fees. Attorneys are quick to point out that certain "minimum charges" for various different probate manipulations tend to run up the cost percentage-wise in smaller estates. However, in almost every case, once an accurate inventory of an estate's assets is laid upon the attorney's desk, the legal costs and fees of probate have the strangest way of expanding to consume the more robust funds available in larger estates as well.

The processing time, paper procedures, and general flux required of the lawyer, judge, secretaries, clerks, and the like, in settling a $600,000 estate closely parallel the exertions of settling a smaller $100,000 estate. Yet, the final statement from the attorney will reflect a charge three or four times higher in the more sizable estate. A commercial carwash that charged $5.00 to wash a Chevrolet and $20.00 to wash a Cadillac would soon hear from the Better Business Bureau.

Further lining the attorney's pockets, if disgruntled or disinherited heirs contest the estate in probate court, the proceedings emerge into a good old-fashioned family donnybrook. These bloody battles often take years to resolve at huge legal costs and attorney fees that have been known to gobble up the entire estate.

Even using the legal profession's modest, attorney-projected probate cost percentages of three to six percent, this all means that if you have a $250,000 estate (modest in this day and age), you can look forward in a non-contested probate to $7,500 to $15,000 of your money seeping down through the courts and attorneys—and eventually through the attorney's estate (attorneys also eventually die) into the pockets of the attorney's children *rather than your own.*

For more than twelve centuries, a conspiring legal profession has deliberately orchestrated this quandary. For more than a millennium, the ruse has succeeded in intimidating grieving and confused families of the recently deceased into the arms of general-practice attorneys who earn up to twenty percent of their annual income by needlessly skimming thousands of dollars off the top of estates.

# THE TRUTH ABOUT YOUR ASSETS: WHICH AVOID PROBATE AND WHICH DON'T

In estate planning we deal basically with tangible assets such as cash, investments, real estate, home furnishings, automobiles, and such. Thus, it is important to understand that for estate-planning purposes you own two different types of tangible assets.

## Assets in Your Physical Possession

Often referred to as "personal property," they would include your household furnishings and equipment, garden and lawn tools, jewelry, heirlooms, inventories of supplies and food, cash either in your pocket or under the mattress, stamp collections, gun collections, grandma's silverware, and similar items. Automobiles, even though they have titles, can also be considered to be personal property and now avoid probate on their own hook in all fifty states. (Automobiles are discussed in chapter 9.)

The security of such assets is your own responsibility. Unless you can afford your own security guard, you are the custodian of your personal property. If any of your personal property is stolen, you have nothing to protect you from loss other than an insurance policy or the quick response of the local police department.

Assets in your possession avoid probate. There will be no sentry standing guard at your front door after you and your spouse die. Such assets have no legal titles and any of your children or relatives can enter your home after you and your spouse are dead and make off with any of these possessions. Who is to say that such assets ever existed? In fact, that is the way it usually works out; the first one there gets the best stuff.

Such personal property raids are often the cause of much family animosity and money-wasting lawsuits for years to come. Jack wanted the piano but Jill got there first. If some of the assets in your possession have special meaning and you want them distributed to special people, you must make some special arrangements such as leaving behind a signed list as to who gets what.

## Assets Not in Your Physical Possession

You probably have deposited larger, more valuable assets in the safe-keeping of various financial custodians (banks, stockbrokers, credit unions, or insurance companies) who are responsible for the safekeeping of the assets. You receive a title or receipt from the financial custodian indicating that they are holding the asset for you. Such assets are almost always cash that take the form of savings accounts, certificates of deposit, stocks, mutual funds, bonds, insurance policies, annuities, and IRA accounts.

Long-standing fiduciary laws prohibit your financial custodians from releasing these assets to anyone, including yourself, without your authorized, written permission. And, of course, you cannot give such written permission after you are dead. Thus rises the question: how do your heirs get those assets out of the banks, credit unions, stockbrokers, and so forth, if you are not around to sign the papers?

## What about Real Estate (Your Home, Your Farm, Etc.)?

Strange as it may seem, homes, farms, and other real estate are also considered to be in that group of assets not in your possession.

In prehistoric times, when a hunting party went out looking for something to eat, two or three tribesmen stayed behind to prevent marauding neighbors from taking physical possession of the tribal cave. Such thievery was a part of the tradition of the times and tended to produce great social unrest and a fair amount of bloodshed.

Thankfully, in a civilized society, the ownership of property has evolved into a system where the former owner of any real estate you purchase gives you a warranty deed that officially transfers the ownership of the property from his name to yours. That deed is invaluable to you. First, it proves that the property was indeed that of the seller and free of encumbrances such as mortgages or back taxes. It also signifies that you are the new owner of that real estate. For your protection, the deed is recorded at the registrar of deeds office in the county or parish in which the property is located. No one can move into your home and claim ownership while you are vacationing in Bermuda or shopping at the mall.

In this way the registrar of deeds office serves to guarantee the ownership of your real property just as a bank guarantees your ownership of your savings account. The property is registered in your name down at the courthouse just as your money is in the bank in an account with your name on it.

## Exceptions to the Rule

Your estate boils down to 1) assets in your physical possession and 2) assets not in your physical possession. Assets in your possession avoid probate while assets not in your possession require probate. Simple, huh?

Well, not quite.

There is one big exception to the rule that you should know about: any asset not in your possession that names a beneficiary on the title of that asset automatically avoids probate. Such assets include life insurance policies, annuities, IRAs, 401K-type investments, pensions, and the like.

> ### Payment on Death Beneficiaries
> Many states now allow you to add a POD or TOD ("payment on death" or "transfer on death") beneficiary to bank accounts, certificates of deposit, stock certificates, mutual funds and brokerage accounts. The beneficiary listed on the title of an asset need only produce your death certificate and positive identification to take possession of the asset in usually forty-eight to seventy-two hours. No probate is needed.

We live in an age where many people hold much of their estates in IRAs, 401Ks, annuities and other assets with beneficiaries listed on the title. Thus, the need for probate is often limited to a surprisingly few number of assets. So why can't you simply leave written instructions authorizing your financial custodians to release such assets (both assets that list beneficiaries on the deeds and titles and assets that have no titles) directly to the individuals that you want to have them?

That is exactly what most responsible persons attempt to do! The instructions are called a Last Will and Testament.

Why then, upon reading the requests of your Last Will and Testament, can't your financial custodians simply release those assets to the heirs named in your will?

Because the banker or other financial custodian has absolutely no idea how many wills you wrote before you died. There very well could be another will out there somewhere that supercedes the one some heir has just handed the financial custodian. If the financial custodian mistakenly gives the asset to the wrong heir, that custodian faces an airtight lawsuit by the rightful heir. Thus, the financial custodian must await probate court's official designation of heirs before it dares release the asset.

And what is it that satisfies the financial custodian's dilemma? Twelve to twenty-four months of legal work and three to fifteen percent skimmed off the top of the estate by some attorney.

## ENTER THE LIVING TRUST

The living trust, which became a part of English Common Law nearly five hundred years ago, does away with the need for probate at death by re-titling your assets so that they seamlessly transfer to your heirs. Until recently, living trusts were covered up by the legal profession and rarely offered as an alternative to clients. This reaction seemed rather strange and inappropriate, considering the living trust is astonishingly simple and no more difficult to achieve than opening a checking account. No attorney is needed to set up a legal living trust, which can be made functional in just two or three days. Not surprisingly, however, most attorneys have found the living trust to be seriously flawed because it seeks to do away with the need of an attorney at death.

Since the publication of Norman Dacey's book, estate-planning attorneys have divided into two camps.

Camp One: Distort the living trust as a complex and costly set of documents, advantageous only to the very wealthy, and which can be legally and safely drawn only by an attorney.

Camp Two: Recoup probate fees lost to the growing popularity of living trusts by jumping on the living trust bandwagon and deliberately writing unnecessarily complex and costly trust documents that at death require the services of the attorney to unscramble.

Thus, hiring a lawyer to draw your living trust may be like hiring a fox to guard your hen house. To keep the cash cow delivering the cream, most attorney-written living trusts are intentionally and unnecessarily complex in order to force the heirs back to the lawyer to unscramble the trust and settle the estate. When the attorney's fee for settling the trust is added to the attorney's exorbitant fee for initially drawing the trust documents themselves, it becomes obvious that the attorney intends to get his fee, regardless of whether the estate avoids probate or not.

# 2

# The Nuts and Bolts of Probate

In America, as in most free countries around the world, a citizen that is of legal age, mentally competent and not in jail is pretty much free to paddle his own canoe as he sees fit. So long as you break no laws you are permitted to handle your own affairs as you choose. You may become very wealthy or you may muck up your business and activities to the extent that you face bankruptcy. You pay your money and make your own decisions.

However, should you be too young, too mentally incapacitated, too physically disabled, or too dead to make choices for yourself, the state in which you reside must step in to protect your interests.

There are three distinct ways in which the probate system can entangle you. First, if you are orphaned, the court must appoint guardians to manage your assets and inheritance until you reach the legal age of eighteen. Second, should you become physically or mentally incapacitated through old age or some bodily tragedy, the court must step in to see for your care. A guardian must be appointed to watch over your physical being, and a conservator or property guardian must be appointed to watch over your assets.

But the most notorious mode in which probate can ensnarl your family occurs after you are dead. You are then in no condition to defend the assets you accumulated during your lifetime nor make any arrangements on your own to deed such assets to your heirs, so probate court must step in to manage an orderly transfer of those assets to the next generation.

## PROBATE AFTER DEATH

According to *The Wall Street Journal*, the average length of time needed by this obsolete system to probate a decedent's estate is nearly eighteen months. And that is if everything runs smoothly! Contested wills (wills that are challenged in probate court by dissatisfied heirs and creditors) can add several years or even a decade to the overall program.

Bill Lear of Learjet fame died in 1978. However, his will remains contested in probate court yet today because of internal errors. Movie screen star John Wayne has been dead since 1979, but his estate lingers on in California probate as relatives compete for his wealth.

One would believe that such multi-millionaires as Mr. Lear and Mr. Wayne would have been able to afford the finest in competent attorneys. Chances are they both had the best, but it did not prevent the estates of either from being torn to ribbons by the legal jackals representing the discontented heirs.

## The Process Begins

Once the probate process has weighed anchor, all the decedent's financial matters are completely in the hands of the judge, the attorney, and the personal representative (often called an executor or executrix) appointed by the decedent in his will. The attorney is almost always the same attorney that wrote the will years before because seldom is the mourning family in any rational mental mode to search for another lawyer. In fact, that was most likely the plan of the attorney that authored the will all along.

Rarely is the family of the decedent granted an audience with the judge; instead, they are forced to seek all official communication with the court through the decedent's personal representative or attorney. Functioning much like an army general, the attorney commissions the lesser-paid, decedent-appointed personal representative to bird-dog the pertinent details of the estate such as digging up an inventory of all the assets, having those assets officially appraised, and, to the best of his ability, tracking down all creditors (and debtors) having a veracious claim against the estate.

To prevent anyone from being overlooked, most states require probate court to place a notice in an accepted county newspaper publicly announcing the decedent's passing and inviting all creditors, real or pretended, along with any dissatisfied or disinherited relatives and friends, to plead their case by attending either the initial court hearing or by contacting the decedent's personal representative.

Anyone and everyone is publicly invited to the estate-raiding festivities. Charlatans can materialize out of nowhere waving five-year-old bills for snow removal or other hard-to-disprove obligations of the deceased.

Often the personal representative finds himself engulfed by the system's out-of-control, rolling snowball and thus simply turns most of his responsibilities over to the attorney. This kicks into gear the politics that undermine the entire process. A hoard of sycophants that dwell just below the surface often arise to line their pockets with drive-by appraisals of real estate and other minor and highly questionable "legal" errands. In smaller counties such toadies are oft times moonlighting real estate agents, insurance agents, and bank clerks looking to add to their regular income. In counties with larger populations, where additional deaths create more probate court action, such friends of the court can be full-time, commission-driven opportunists.

The probate judgeship in itself is an elected position to be determined by the voters usually every four years. However, it often becomes a political plum that is among the spoils handed out by a victorious new state governor. As a matter of fact, the voters in most of the counties of America have not had an opportunity in years to make a free choice between competitive newcomers for a probate judgeship. The governor's

*If law school is so hard to get through…how come there are so many lawyers?*

—CALVIN TRILLIN

fresh appointee generally settles in for a long incumbency, frequently running unopposed for re-election term after term. While running the NCAP, I've watched a shameful number of elections in Michigan and nearby states where the incumbent runs unopposed not only for probate judgeships, but also for circuit judgeships, district judgeships, and municipal judgeships. Where I live, in Barry County, Michigan, there has only been one election in the past thirty years where two political newcomers vied for a judgeship (in this case it was District Court).

Few attorneys want to risk their influence with the court by challenging the judge for his job. As the years fly by and incumbents get a bit long in the tooth, many find it "necessary" to resign before finishing out their final terms. The process then repeats as the governor rewards a new brownnoser—sometimes from another corner of the state—with the appointment to "fill the un-expired term." Thus, the new magistrate has a couple of years to get his feet on the ground and his name in the newspapers and social register before facing the voters as an incumbent.

Neither the court nor its officers are in the habit of exercising much discretion or frugality when it comes to spending someone else's money. And to be sure, nothing is forgotten. As mentioned earlier, in addition to the attorney's fee, the estate will be charged for every appointment made by the court, every hearing, every letter of authority, every safety deposit box opening, every jurist and every stenographer fee, right down to the last telephone call and postage stamp. Only the salaries of the judge and his assistants are paid by the county's taxpayers.

## Minimum Requirements for Probate

While many states set a $30,000 to $60,000 estate minimum as a requirement for probate, in others the law is quite vague. The judge has full discretion, and, in the case of very small estates ($4,000 to $5,000) the judge may, without further notice or hearing, turn over directly to the spouse what little funds are left after burial expenses, court costs, and attorney fees are paid. On the other hand, a single asset worth $5,000 to $10,000 can trigger the entire trappings of the system and expose a distraught and destitute widow or widower to a year or more of costly and agonizing court procedure.

## Will Contests

Should the personal representative be unable to negotiate a satisfactory settlement with creditors and discontents, their claims and complaints are turned over to the judge who must act as a referee as to the legitimacy of those demands. Should the judge be unable to make a final determination during the initial court hearing, she must call additional hearings—again at the expense of the estate—to resolve the matters.

Nationally, a third of the wills contested by dissatisfied heirs and relatives are overturned and the terms of the distribution altered by the judge. Because it is the business of probate court to settle such altercations expediently, disenfranchised heirs can often plead their case—at least in the early stages of the probate procedure—without personal legal counsel. The fact that in such litigations the disappointed heir faces no initial attorney fee often proves to be an additional incentive for challenging a will.

People are free to leave their property to anyone they choose, so incompetence or duress at the time of drawing the will are the only grounds for contesting a will. However, this seldom deters disappointed kinfolk. Challenges to a decedent's will are usually made on the weakest of foundations with little or no chance of winning. Aware of the frustration he will cause by months of wrangling in court, the adversary's strategy is to jam the gears of any final settlement—thus bringing the legal heirs to their knees in hope that they will "cut a deal" outside of court and prevent the further financial drain of court costs and attorney fees upon the estate. Those who believe that their attorney will aggressively fight off the disputes of disinherited relatives often fail to realize that it makes little difference financially to the attorney as to who will inherit and who will not. Probate laws of most states allow the attorney be paid off the top of the estate—even before the undertaker and the tax collector—thus, it makes little difference to the attorney if there is anything left for the heirs. After all, a bit of sporting competition and dissension in the courtroom serves to run up the tab.

## Lack of Privacy

The fact that all probate records and hearings are open to the public can be most troublesome for the family. Private rifts and family skeletons often stand naked to the public eye. Iniquitous and unprincipled solicitors with "can't miss" investment schemes, financial management ploys, and Brooklyn Bridge fire sales often take advantage of the open books of probate to prey on soon-to-inherit widows and orphans.

Prospective decedents who wish to keep their private financial affairs under wraps after death can jolly well guess again. Every bank balance, every loan, and every default are exposed to anyone who cares to amble in off the street and examine the records. Hoping to unearth a front-page sensation that will raise the circulation a thousand or two, newspaper editors usually assign reporters with a nose for news to the probate beat.

## Unavailability of Assets

Once the court has had the opportunity to review all bills and possible taxes due from the estate, it may well determine that there is sufficient financial strength within the estate to order a reasonable living allowance to a widow(er) and possibly to the small children. But in general, most assets and investments are frozen during the probate procedure. A declining market can raise havoc with stocks and securities incarcerated in the paralysis of probate. Medical and dental needs, inoperative vehicles, and business and investment opportunities of the immediate family often must await the final gavel by the judge. There are thousands of horror stories such as children being forced to drop out of college because educational funds provided during the lifetime of the decedent, resting in properly earmarked savings accounts, are tied up in the static world of probate.

### A Cautionary Tale

One of the most frustrating situations I've encountered at the NCAP was a documented Michigan case in which a young man and his wife were completing the last phases of building a house. They had paid the builder out of their own savings for much of the work and had the agreement of the young man's widowed father that he would stake the couple to the final twenty-five percent of the building cost and take a personal note. However, the father met with a tragic and life-terminating car accident on the day the house was completed. The father had no will and his estate as of this writing is still tied up in a long and complex intestate probate process. The builder attached the house with a Mechanic's Lien and the couple is in danger of losing their life savings—all due to the fact that the father had not taken proper care of his estate when he had the chance.

Should liquid assets (assets that are quickly converted to cash, such as stocks, bonds, mutual funds, and certificates of deposit) be inadequate to cover all due bills and taxes, the judge has the power to order the decedent's real estate and personal property sold to meet the expense. On the long drainpipe of asset distribution, the legal heirs crowd anxiously together under the very last spigot.

Be aware also that the family will be in line for an additional treat should it be discovered that the decedent holds title to real estate located somewhere other than her state of residence. The entire probate process must be repeated in another state under a different set of probate regulations with a fresh new attorney licensed to practice in that state.

The probate procedure at death can be compared to a taxicab ride in a large and unfamiliar city. Who among us has not had the dubious delight of sitting in the back seat of a taxi—block after block, stoplight after stoplight, traffic jam after traffic jam—helplessly watching the fare advance upward at fifty cents a click. We may be convinced that the cabdriver has spotted us for the rube that we are and is intentionally going miles out of the way to line his own pockets. Yet to question his knowledge of the city would probably serve only to expose our ignorance, and to change cabs might catapult us from the frying pan into the fire. Thus we choose to remain silent, stare at the mounting tariff, and hope that we can recover from this unexpected compound fracture to our budget. The ride through probate is astonishingly analogous!

## Economy-Size Probate

Actually you may be able to dispense with a part of this ride. States having approved a revised Uniform Probate Code make available a stream-lined version of the probate process called Independent or Unsupervised Probate. Attorneys advertise this as a more economical and timesaving edition. If the estate is a simple one (in which there is little or no debt and most assets are liquid enough to quickly convert to cash) the entire procedure can be handled by an attorney and personal representative without court supervision. Since attorney and personal representative fees represent the lion's share of the overall cost, dumping the involvement of the court itself should eliminate perhaps thirty percent of the total probate time and toll. Understand that Independent or Unsupervised Probate is relatively new. Not enough time or experience has passed under the bridge to determine if the public is actually receiving a thirty-percent reduction in probate costs, or if attorneys are pocketing a part of the savings. One thing is for sure: the opportunity for an attorney to skim off a portion of the saved funds through increasing her fee is certainly present.

*"Where there's a will, there's an Inheritance Tax."*

—UNKNOWN

In some ways this so-called compressed aberration of probate is an exacerbation of the standard model. Because the court is not involved and there is no public agency to broadcast the decedent's affairs to creditors and other interested parties, direct notices listing the decedent's assets and private business are mailed by the personal representative to all possible heirs and creditors. In other words, the law provides that if newspaper advertising can't do the job of blabbing a family's private financial affairs all over town, a little direct mail will put the particulars right on the desktop of every long-lost relative, neighbor, and creditor.

This abbreviated, fast-forwarded version of probate can also backfire. Dissatisfied heirs and creditors who feel that they are being railroaded out of their respective inheritances and payments of debt can force probate court to open old-fashioned, formal hearings. In the end, the whole procedure is forced back to square one, adding to the overall cost. Remember, regardless of which variant is used, the attorney and the personal representative always get their cut.

## Dying Without a Will

Enough of the good news! What you have read thus far is a reasonable projection of some of the adventures that await those who prepare as best they can for the ordeals of probate court by dying *testate* (having drawn a legal and binding Last Will and Testament before death).

Shockingly, seventy percent of the rank and file depart this world intestate (having made no legal or binding Last Will and Testament before death). What motivates people to ignore this eventuality? Procrastination? Indifference? Lethargy? Don't-feed-it-and-maybe-it-will-go-away-itis? Whatever the reason for this neglect, the breach of dying without a will opens a brand-new can of worms. And if the surviving family of a testate decedent has absolutely no control or privacy during the probate circus, the heirs of a decedent who chooses to go to his grave without leaving a will have even less dominion—if such a thing is possible!

In the case of intestate death, the state's probate system, rather than being cast in the role of referee, becomes a hard-nosed dictator. Now it is the judge who gets to choose the attorney and the personal representative—a practice which all too often turns into a mutual back-scratching exercise with old law partners and friends.

Once a court-appointed attorney and executor are in place, the process of ferreting out and appraising the assets, locating the creditors, and paying the bills and taxes is much the same as in the already described scenario of dying testate. However, when the intestate decedent has left not a single clue as to her desires, the legal costs mount much more rapidly as the executor of the estate and the court blindly attempt to find and fit all the pieces together.

## Personal Performance Bonds

The executor (or personal representative) must furnish a personal performance bond. This bond is a guarantee, put up by a bonding company, that should the executor take off with some or all of the estate money or make a mistake that costs an heir a part of her inheritance, the bond company will reimburse the estate. The maker of a will can always formally request that the personal representative serve without this expensive personal performance bond, but in the absence of such a request the executor of the estate is forced by law to furnish one. This bond can amount to several hundred dollars or even several thousand dollars (depending on the size of the estate), a cost that is charged against the estate.

> **State of the Union**
> In the case of an intestate decedent, state statutes dictate property distribution. In Michigan, a widow receives the first $60,000 and fifty percent of the balance. The children receive the other fifty percent in equal shares. Should there be no widow and/or no children, the assets follow a very complex path to more distant relatives that would take or three pages of a book to explain. Interestingly, in Michigan, a husband has no marital rights.

*They all laid their heads together like as many lawyers when they are gettin' ready to prove that a man's heirs ain't got any right to his property.*

—MARK TWAIN

At a final distribution concluding an intestate probate procedure, the dictatorial powers of state law become absolute and inflexible. The residue from assets left after all fees, costs, taxes, and debts are paid is distributed to the heirs according to an ironclad state formula. Absolutely no consideration is given to what is subjective, equitable, or moral. Only the hard-core rules of the state are considered.

The complex and concrete-etched statutes regulating the distribution of the estate of an intestate decedent vary greatly from state to state. Generally speaking, however, the surviving spouse (should there be one) is awarded a fixed amount or percentage of the estate. Legal children of the couple (should there be any) receive the balance in equal shares. If there are no children, the balance of the assets wiggle their way over a complicated path to siblings, parents, aunts, uncles, nephews, nieces, and cousins. It matters not that the spouse requires all of the estate to maintain even the most frugal lifestyle or that the first of two children is an impoverished invalid and the other child has a successful profession and estate of her own valued in the millions. Each child will inherit an equal share as the law provides. It might be that one child is a scoundrel who the decedent booted out of the home years ago. It matters not; she will inherit equally with her brothers and sisters.

This unbending method of asset distribution in intestate deaths is tailor-made for family dissension, feuding, and bitter resentment. Yet, the law remains unsympathetic and intractable. To the discernment of probate court the matter is closed. Call the next case.

## A COMPARISON OF INTESTATE AND TESTATE PROBATE PROCEDURES

| Intestate Probate | Testate Probate |
| --- | --- |
| ▶ Decedent has no Last Will and Testament | ▶ Decedent has a Last Will and Testament |
| ▶ Attorney required in most cases | ▶ Attorney usually required but can occasionally be probated privately by heirs |
| ▶ Personal representative required | ▶ Personal representative required |
| ▶ Minimum time required: depends upon the state in which the estate is probated | ▶ Minimum time required: depends upon the state in which the estate is probated |
| ▶ Average time required: 15 to 30 months | ▶ Average time required: 12 to 24 months |
| ▶ Open to all challenges by heirs and creditors | ▶ Open to all challenges by heirs and creditors |
| ▶ Distribution of assets as per incontestable marital laws of the state involved. Decedent's verbal wishes while alive are not considered | ▶ Distribution of assets as per the conditions written in the Last Will and Testament, upon approval of judge |
| ▶ Cost: 3 to 15 percent of the gross estate, before obligations of the estate are considered | ▶ Cost: 3 to 15 percent of the gross estate, before obligations of the estate are considered |

# PROBATE: DEAD OR ALIVE!

Wait! There is more! In the beginning I told you that in addition to death, the probate system has other ways of embroiling you under its heat and, in most such cases, you will find yourself to be very much alive.

Should you become physically or mentally incapacitated or incompetent, you will doubtlessly be placed under the control of a probate court–appointed conservator (a person appointed by the court to handle all financial matters of a person legally judged to be underage or mentally incompetent). Often the court designates a family member as conservator, however the judge is free to appoint anyone she chooses, such as an attorney or a person totally unfamiliar with the family's history or present situation. But even if the conservator is a family member, he is answerable to and under the control of the court and its unyielding rules.

As in the case of someone deceased, the system is built to protect the assets of those mentally or physically unable to handle their own affairs. That you will not fritter away your possessions, probate court stands ready to administer your personal property and real estate should you be unable to conduct your own affairs competently, or you are unwilling to relinquish control. The conservator is paid a flat rate or commission from the estate. Often the conservator is a professional who makes a business out of managing the assets of several estates at the same time.

In addition to a conservator, the court will also appoint a *personal guardian* for the incompetent or incapacitated person. In the case of all incapacitated adults (as well in regard to minors, to be discussed shortly), it takes two to tango. A personal guardian must be appointed to the physical care of the incapacitated person, and a court-controlled conservator must be appointed to manage the funds and assets. The incompetent person (while coherent) can only recommend or elect her choice of nominees for these jobs. It is probate court that puts the final stamp of approval on these selections.

Loss of physical or mental control of one's faculties is of increasing concern in this country. As the years of life expectancy continue to grow with the advances in medicine, longer life spans expose us to the danger of at least a few years of incapacity before we pass from this world. Without proper planning, a court-appointed conservatorship becomes a definite potentiality for everyone.

And it is important to note that the inability to function competently can strike at any age. A catastrophic illness or a calamitous accident can leave you alive, but without the capability to perform on a limited basis. Such a cataclysm can be most devastating to a young couple that has mistakenly tried to beat the system by placing all their property and possessions in co-ownership (a type of multi-ownership called *joint tenancy* that will be discussed fully in chapter 3).

As an example: Tim and Dorothy have a large, young, and hungry family to feed, shelter, and educate. Tim survives a serious automobile accident, but is left in a wheelchair, permanently brain-damaged and nearly helpless. As the sole breadwinner, Dorothy must raise money for living expenses and education and will have to sell the house and move to a smaller, more affordable home. Dorothy would like to care for Tim privately at home with no interference from the court or county services. However, Tim and Dorothy's present home and securities are in the co-ownership of joint tenancy, with both names appearing on the titles. Because Tim is unable to sign his name or comprehend the consequences of his actions, Dorothy is forced to place Tim in a probate conservatorship for what in this case will be a lifelong arrangement in order to gain the authority to sell her husband's share of the jointly-owned, titled assets. Don't look to Dorothy to be appointed conservator. The judge usually will reward someone from his own group of legal friends to enjoy this bauble.

*Death and taxes and childbirth! There's never any convenient time for any of them!*

—MARGARET MITCHELL

# Power of Attorney

To explode another popular myth, many people believe that at such times their carefully drawn Last Will and Testament can save their chestnuts. Persons named in their will, such as a guardian or possibly the executor, can step in at such a burdensome time to deal with the per diem chores. However, a will is but a simple laundry list of wishes that can become effectual only upon death and, even then, only after months of probate procedure. While an incapacitated person remains alive, their Last Will and Testament is a useless piece of paper tucked away in a bureau drawer or a lawyer's safe.

There are also those who believe that giving a trusted friend or relative legal written permission to act as one's agent (known as a *power of attorney*) while alive to be the solution. However, standard power of attorney becomes invalid upon incompetency or death. *Durable* power of attorney, available in some states, remains valid during any period of incompetency, but is also revoked upon death.

*Attorneys-in-fact* (persons who have been given power of attorney) are most practical and useful in the routine financial operations of day-to-day life, such as writing checks, making bank deposits, signing contracts, and conducting the purchase and sale of assets and supplies. However, since the giving of durable power of attorney can be an open invitation to deception and the looting of an estate, few people are willing to grant attorneys-in-fact the limitless agency powers needed to act unchecked in all situations and emergencies. It must also be remembered that vendors and financial institutions are under no obligation to honor a power of attorney any more than they have an obligation to do business with you. In fact, many banks and stock-brokers do not recognize a power of attorney given outside of their own institutions. Thus, should the court declare one legally incompetent, a judge-appointed conservator typically oversees the disbursement of all funds. While the judge may appoint one's agent as conservator, he is under no obligation to do so; he may ignore the power of attorney and appoint whomever he pleases.

## Declaring a Person Incompetent

Anyone can file a petition with the court to have a person declared incompetent. A friend, relative, or even a next-door neighbor whose observations evidence a person behaving in an irresponsible or erratic manner can initiate a competency hearing in probate court. Tragically, however, the original motion is often made by some unconscionable relative with designs on being named conservator, thereby enabling that relative to gain control of the incompetent person's wealth. Such probate court hearings have been known to drag on for months or years until either legal fees dissipate the person's wealth or the petitioner's patience is exhausted.

Should the allegedly incompetent person choose to attend the hearing(s), the experience is often one of great humiliation and tearful debasement. In a well-remembered televised misfortune of the 1970s, famed comic Groucho Marx, in a wheelchair, sat in a courtroom for months, weeping and disgraced, as the woman he lived with tried to persuade the judge that the aged vaudevillian and movie star really wanted her rather than a relative as conservator.

Once the ball of a competency hearing is put in play, the agenda is much the same as that of probating a will. The hearing is advertised in the legal section of a county newspaper to allow creditors the opportunity to present their bills. The judge appoints an attorney on behalf of the allegedly incapacitated person, and, in keeping with the laws of most states, that attorney must advise him of his rights and the time and place of the hearing. Should the person choose not to challenge the petition, the attorney reports her findings as to the person's physical health and mental well being to the court.

Should the judge (or jury if so ordered) rule the person incompetent, a conservator is appointed. The person judged mentally unfit not only loses control of his money and assets but also forfeits most of his rights as an American citizen. The conservator inventories the assets and liabilities and submits the list, along with a proposed living expense budget, to the court for approval. The conservator is entitled to fair compensation for his work (determined by the judge) and the judge may order the property and possessions of the person judged incompetent sold at public auction to pay present and future expenses.

Through an attorney, the conservator must make a complete and comprehensive report on the case back to the court once a year. However, in some cases the court is so grossly understaffed as to the monitoring of the conservatorship that after a period of years the assets just disappear, vanishing in the mist of mismanagement.

The court-controlled conservatorship is an ongoing legal status that can terminate only with the recovery or the death of the incompetent person. Recovery, at least from the legal standpoint, is difficult if not downright impossible. Should you be the unfortunate victim, you are usually tucked far away in a nursing home from where you, on your own initiative, must reverse the entire legal procedure by first petitioning the court to hear the case and then retaining several professionals (psychiatrists, psychologists, and so forth) to attest to your recovery. Finally, you must wheedle the court into believing that you can now care for yourself.

From a practical standpoint you can probably look forward to scant assistance from your family in any such legal battle because they will justifiably be apprehensive that any error in the court's judgment might force your personal custody and financial responsibility back on them. Furthermore, it is very often that a family member initiated the hearings to declare you incompetent in the first place.

Failure to reverse your incompetent status sentences you to a lonely death still chained to the caste of incapacity. Upon your demise, the conservatorship is closed and a new file is opened. Should there be no will, an executor is appointed, newspaper readers—including any remaining creditors—are advised of your passing, and what's left of your estate is admitted to guess where? Probate!

> *I enjoyed the courtroom as just another stage— but not so amusing as Broadway.*
>
> —MAE WEST

## PROBATE PROTECTION FOR MINORS

Let's now move on to another path leading into the hallowed halls of probate—a path that concerns children of minor age.

Other than savings and checking accounts, personal effects, and the clothes on their backs, minor children cannot hold property titled solely in their own names. Thus, should a person under eighteen years of age receive benefits from a life insurance policy or IRA-type of savings, become a joint owner of property, or inherit real estate, stocks, bonds, or other assets, the interests of that child must be protected by the state's probate system.

Now for another popular myth: many parents believe that, upon the death of both parents, a personal guardian named in a will can step in spontaneously and, using the child's inheritance, rear the child to adulthood.

Not true.

One of the responsibilities of the court as it probates the surviving parent's estate is to appoint a personal guardian for any minor children involved. Should the decedent have nominated a guardian in her will, the judge will take that recommendation under advisement. However, the court is under no obligation to appoint the decedent's choice. Should the deceased's preference of guardians seem to be unstable, the court may well choose someone else who it feels is better qualified.

The personal guardian physically rears and cares for the underage children, while a court-controlled property guardian or conservator manages the funds and assets. If the decedent has died without making such nominations in a will, the court, which then has no idea of the decedent's wishes or if indeed the decedent even cared, is free to make both choices as it desires. However, these decisions are of the utmost importance: custody of the child is given to the decedent-nominated and court-approved personal guardian, yet the control of the money from the inheritance remains with the court through that person appointed as conservator.

Two factors here are important to remember. There are few persons standing in line willing to physically rear and shelter someone else's children to adulthood. Thus, the court will generally place its blessing on almost any responsible person you nominate for the position. However, the job of conservator is an entirely different story. There are many people in the county anxious to be given the job of handling someone else's money and a judge usually has a list of his own personal favorites. Nonetheless, the personal nomination of someone for conservator in your will is a way of at least getting your two cents in.

The child's court-appointed property guardian, entitled to be compensated out of the child's inheritance, is required to post a security bond and must hire an attorney to submit to the court an annual

*Lawyers,*
*I suppose, were*
*children once.*

—CHARLES LAMB

detailed report of the child's income and disbursements. Any expenditure over and above the approved minimum living allowance must be submitted to the court in writing by an attorney.

Our modern society understands and acknowledges each individual to be a distinctive being with her own personality and requirements. However, under probate's austere laws, the court is obliged to treat each juvenile alike. A child's unique aptitude and talents often go ignored by an understaffed court or the antiquated approach of a judge. The loss of both parents is a hard blow to any child's confidence and self-esteem. Further prohibition of such things in a young person's life as club memberships, school and social activities, excursions, athletic participation, dancing lessons, bicycles, and so forth that give the child a sense of belonging and homogenizing with her peers can retard or shade a child's personality development for years to come. However, for the most part, the court must remain adamant in its inflexible stance.

Sapient parents often see fit to dole out a large inheritance to a child over a period of years in several installments. However, when probate court is running the show, court control ceases when the child reaches legal age. By law, the court is forced to hand over what is left of the child's inheritance in one lump sum. Regardless of the child's degree of maturity or lack of financial seasoning and responsibility, this new legal adult, still a fiscal babe in the woods, is sent forth into the world to do as he pleases with the first real money he has ever possessed. Too often a long-denied, yet immature orphan rapidly squanders the windfall on sports cars and fancy togs.

But what if the child is not orphaned? Let's go back to our friends, Tim and Dorothy, for a moment to illustrate an even more intolerable predicament. Let's suppose that both spouses are incapacitated by that auto accident. Each of them may have made provisions within their wills to set up a private guardianship or children's trust (to be discussed in Chapter 7) which will avoid a court-appointed guardian and conservator. However, no one has died! Their wills cannot kick into gear to activate the provisions within them. Such a family crisis could remain in a state of limbo for months and probably would be resolved by placing both incapacitated parents and their minor children in a court-appointed and administrated conservatorship or guardianship.

*If only God would give me some clear sign! Like making a large deposit in my name at a Swiss bank.*

—WOODY ALLEN

### Minor Inheritances

There is even a way that minors can end up under the control of the court when both parents are healthy, happy, gainfully employed, and living together! Any money, real estate, certificates of deposit, stocks or other investments bequeathed to minors in the will of other well-meaning relatives (such as grandparents, older siblings, aunts, and uncles) will automatically involve the probate system. Once again, *minor children cannot inherit directly.* The court must appoint a conservator—who in many instances will be the child's parent. However, the aggravation value of having to hire an attorney at a fee of perhaps three hundred dollars per year to report to the court until the child reaches legal age can prove to be exasperating.

Because of possible liability problems, insurance companies will rarely make disbursements directly to a minor who has been named the beneficiary of an insurance policy. Adults who wish to name their underage children as beneficiaries of their life insurance policies should arrange to name a children's trust as beneficiary. The court will still be involved with the approval of the trustee of such a trust, however this is generally just a formality. No further court "assistance" is required.

## PROBATE MARCHES ON . . . AND ON . . . AND ON

So this is a capsule of probate. It remains today in much the same form as it did a millennium ago. Its regulations and procedures linger on as if they were chiseled in the marble arch over the courthouse door. Though faster, more efficient, and far less expensive systems of transferring assets to heirs and administering to the needs of minors and the incompetent have existed for centuries, the legal profession continues to conceal them from public view and knowledge.

Also, it is a fair assertion that a nearly universal social apprehension of death lingers. It remains a conundrum that a society that so verbosely avows a deep spiritual preparedness for a journey into the hereafter fails to witness its conviction with any intensity of discernible financial bag packing. Too often surviving loved ones are stuck with mopping up an amplitude of procrastination and trepidation.

Yet, as you will see in later chapters, a great many of our day-to-day mechanisms, customs, and procedures now accepted as sacred standards for handling private and commercial legal transactions have been molded by the make-work ethic of the legal profession. Like the dentist who never drills the last cavity, conventional legal techniques in place for centuries have turned many a law office into a revolving door for clients who were under the assumption that all their legal problems were solved last month.

The probate system needlessly takes millions of dollars in cold hard cash out of the pockets of American families every day for legal costs and fees. Approximately two-thirds of the measurable financial extraction from an estate finds its way into the saddlebags of the attorneys; the rest goes for court costs and personal representative fees. However, there is no way to put a price tag on the frustration and anxiety it creates in the families it serves. Chagrined by his own profession's rapacious approach to probate, the late Robert F. Kennedy, Attorney General of the United States, opined that "the American probate system has degenerated into nothing more than a tollgate for widows and orphans; a license to rob them of the very funds they need to survive."

The probate system has often been called "the attorney's private retirement fund" and, over London Broil, it is an accepted luncheon pastime for lawyers to banter back and forth about just who among them has the greatest number of wills stashed in the bottom drawer of his file or safe. Many make an entire career from the probating of wills and the managing of guardianships. Others find it commensurate with baseball's American League designated hitter structure. Trial lawyers who have advanced in years and find they have lost a step or two as courtroom shortstops can extend their professional pursuits another decade or so by resorting to the lucrative field of probate.

*"A lawyer with a briefcase can steal more than a thousand men with guns."*

—MARIO PUZO,
*THE GODFATHER*

Because the law requires that a nonprofessional personal representative or executor capable of doing the heavy legwork be assigned to each estate in probate, an attorney can dispatch several wills through probate simultaneously without giving up too many Thursday afternoons on the golf links.

Of course, this foolproof probate tollgate dispenses into the attorney's bank account even before the legal heirs get to touch any of their inheritances. Judges—many of whom have been hungry attorneys themselves—see to it that the attorneys get their fees. Thus, there are no receivables to handle and no arm-twisting collectors to employ; just nice, thick gravy right up front.

The fee charged by the attorney must meet with the court's approval; however, attorneys are predisposed to come up with all sorts of "extraordinary" charges for mileage, telephone conferences, business luncheons, and stationery costs which the judge is only too happy to pass along to the estate and the long-suffering family. The fees set by the court, which attorneys gleefully point to as evidence of a court-regulated price scale, are in actuality *minimum* charges. When final accounting time comes, the attorney charges the maximum fee he thinks the client can afford while the court looks the other way.

## LAWYERS: THICK AS THIEVES

Today, lawyers are everywhere. Not only do attorneys hold down most of the elected federal and state legislative jobs in Washington, D.C., and the various state capitals, there are an additional sixty thousand lawyers employed by the federal government alone and hundreds of thousands more employed by the nation's largest corporations. Most of the corporate attorneys are on the payroll for the sole purpose of opposing the sixty thousand attorneys feeding from the public trough.

Today's laws are penned by attorneys to be deciphered by other attorneys. Legal corruption and roguery is rampant in every state of the union because the legal profession has chosen to be self-regulatory and set itself above the law. When a citizen is wronged by a member of the bar there is absolutely nowhere to go for a remedy, because attorneys all

> ### Complaints against Attorneys
>
> Recently, a story appeared in the *Grand Rapids Press* in regard to complaints against Michigan attorneys. It stated that of Michigan's thirty thousand attorneys, less than fifty are convicted of malpractice in any one year and only two or three are actually disbarred. To read this, one would have to believe that Michigan attorneys are as pure as the driven snow. The problem was that the reporter did not mention how many complaints are filed yearly against Michigan attorneys: according to the state bar hearing records, between seven and eight thousand! That's approximately one complaint for every four attorneys.

look after each other's welfare. Thousands of documented complaints are filed annually with the bar associations of each state. The hearing records of the state bars generally show that those fellow attorneys sitting in judgement of the accused either ignore the malfeasance entirely or deliver a slap on the wrist and send the offending attorney back to his practice to pillage and plunder some more. Less than ten percent of the offending attorneys are found guilty and less than one percent are disbarred. A county prosecutor with a conviction record such as this would find himself out of a job after the next election.

In the case of probate, many months of patience will be rewarded somewhere down the line as the court finally makes distribution of what is left of the assets. Family members are usually so delighted to escape the clutches of the system that they seldom look back over their shoulders to complain about the frustration, humiliation, and price of such a trying and antediluvian practice.

A testate decedent, should he be able to return from the grave for only a few minutes, would be hard pressed to equate the final disbursement of his affairs with the aspirations of his Last Will and Testament. He would look back on the seemingly insignificant attorney fee of perhaps two hundred fifty dollars to draw his will as simply a tool of entrapment that would eventually hazard his family to the exorbitant legal fees, high court costs, molasses-like delays, and general consternation of probate. Viewing the proceedings as a whole, he would vow to follow a different plan in his next life upon this planet.

Such a plan does exist. The procedure is legal, ethical, uncomplicated, private, infinitely less costly, and has been in use for hundreds of years. People from all stations of life and all plateaus of wealth have availed themselves of the strategy not only to conserve their assets for the utility of future generations, but also to ease family pain and strain at their own dissolution. All of these benefits form the backbone for the ever-growing resentment and personal abandonment of America's out-of-date probate system, in favor of the dexterous and simple living trust.

# 3

# Disjointing Joint Tenancy

For many years it has been believed that holding assets in joint tenancy will allow the decedent's estate to bypass the headaches and red tape of the probate process and flow directly to the joint owner. On the surface this is true; however, just underneath that serene and placid veneer is a termite nest of problems that turns joint tenancy (also known as joint ownership) into little more than fool's gold.

## JOINT TENANCY WITH RIGHT OF SURVIVORSHIP

Under Joint Tenancy with Right of Survivorship or its first cousin, Joint Tenancy by the Entirety, two or more people are able to share ownership of an asset. The name of each joint owner appears on the title or deed of the asset. When one of the joint owners (tenants) dies, ownership of the asset automatically re-divides and the decedent's share of the asset flows in equal shares at the moment of death to the surviving co-owners listed on the asset titles. Last man (or woman) standing ends up owning the asset in sole ownership. Bank accounts, stocks, bonds, CDs, real estate, and other assets that list co-owners on their titles pass immediately to the survivor(s). The surviving co-owner on a parcel of real estate need only show up at the registrar of deeds office with a death certificate in hand to have the real estate re-titled solely into her own name.

While the joint tenants are alive, assets in co-ownership are said to be indivisible. For example, should two people co-own an orchard, each co-owner would own half of each tree rather than half the total number of trees in the orchard.

The arrangement is generally an adequate one when made between spouses. In the case of the death of one spouse, the property does pass directly to the surviving spouse, eluding the agony of probate court. But do you know what happens when the surviving spouse eventually dies? Unless he or she remarries and enters into a new joint tenancy with a new wife or husband, joint tenancy terminates with the death of the first spouse to die. Later, at the death of the widow or widower, when there is no one else left on the asset titles to which the assets can automatically pass, the entire estate must then be probated. Children for whom the estate is ultimately destined are never protected from the probate process by the joint tenancy of their parents. Instead, when the surviving spouse dies they become the ultimate victims.

One of the legal profession's most infamous breaches of faith is in advising a client that she can avoid the probate process simply by placing her assets in joint tenancy. No one more than the attorney realizes that such a tale is a classic half-truth. However, the attorney also realizes that since the wife commonly outlives her husband by five to ten years, the estate will usually continue to grow after her husband's death, if by no other means than inflation. When the survivor also dies, the estate must be probated before assets can pass to the children. Not only will the attorney still get to probate the estate, but he will also be entitled to a piece of a much larger pie. Best of all, there will be no one left alive to accuse the attorney of blatant deception. To confirm this, once again put this book down and call your attorney. Ask him again point blank: "Will the assets you suggested that I put in joint ownership with my spouse avoid probate when the surviving spouse dies?" Again, you'll have him between a rock and a hard place.

*No matter how rich you become, how famous or powerful, when you die the size of your funeral will still pretty much depend on the weather.*

—MICHAEL PRITCHARD

## JOINT OWNERSHIP WITH CHILDREN

Choosing to enter joint tenancy with a child is even more foolhardy. First of all, placing assets in joint tenancy with children can bring on a battery of future tax problems for the child, which will be discussed later in this chapter. However, the more camouflaged dangers result from the fact that many parents look on such an alteration of title to their possessions as a gimmick with which to "beat the system" and do not realize the ramifications of what they are actually doing.

## High Risk, Low Reward

You cannot add asterisks to a deed or title noting that the purpose of the joint ownership shown with your spouse or children on the title is to dupe the government and tax collectors, and that the property still really belongs one hundred percent to you. Regardless of any "closet covenant" or under-the-table verbal contract, an adult child given joint tenancy on the title or deed of any asset becomes an equal and legal owner of that asset. The child then has the legal right to access and enjoy that asset and to exercise his equal control to do with the asset as he might choose. The parent has lost her undisputed authority to control the asset.

Should the property be a bank account or certificate of deposit, it is possible for the child to head for the bank, withdraw the entire amount (or cash in the certificate of deposit) and then skip the country. Should the property be the parent's homestead, the child can legally move in—along with furniture, kids, and spouse—or, if refused such access, can create such intolerable legal conditions that the parent is forced to move out or look for a buyer. If selling the property seems to be the only feasible answer to the anguish between parent and child, the child can refuse to sign off his legal share of the home, gutting the whole deal. And, in the case of lawsuits or legal judgments against the child, the property can be attached by the child's creditors.

Consider also that should property be in joint tenancy with several children scattered to the far corners of the country, all papers will need to be shuttled from one child to the next before any sale of property can be consummated by their parents back home. Any one of the children can squelch the sale by refusing to sign off her ownership of the property.

There is also the dilemma of parents who have gotten along beautifully with all their children only to wake up to the verity that their oldest son is having a private tiff with their youngest daughter. Afraid that the consummation of some pending family deal might benefit the other, the siblings cut off not only their own noses but also the prospect of an important sale for mom and dad. Keep in mind that spouses are generally entitled to a "dowry right" of around fifty percent of the estate, depending on the state of residence (marital rights laws differ with almost every state). Therefore, should the children with whom you hold joint tenancy in property be married, their spouses will also have to sign off their rights of inheritance to a portion of the property. This means that joint tenancy with children involves not just blood relatives, but also their spouses, which can open the doors to even more veiled internal family animosity.

## Other Complications

There are other scenarios regarding joint tenancy that are very much worth mentioning. Should an unexpected accident render a child holding joint tenancy in your property incompetent, it will be necessary for you to go through probate to have your own property returned to you in order for you to sell the property. Remote but also very real is the possibility that you and your spouse may die simultaneously (as in an auto accident). Though such a tragedy was not part of your plans and neither of you had provided a will to back up your joint tenancy arrangement, the laws of most states say that if it cannot be determined which spouse died first, or should the surviving spouse die within 72 to 120 hours of the death of the first spouse, the entire estate may have to pass through the misery of a double intestate probate proceeding. This places the final distribution of your assets now exclusively in the hands of the court rather than your heirs. Since most couples that choose joint ownership as an estate plan place everything in their estate in joint tenancy, this results in a double hardship for the surviving family and a double bonanza for the attorney.

And, as Oliver Hardy would say to Stan Laurel: here is another fine mess. Seeking to avoid probate, a widow puts the assets of her estate in joint tenancy with a trusted elder child who agrees to divide the estate evenly with his underage siblings after the mother is gone. The eventual death of the widow is followed a few weeks later by the unexpected death of the elder child. According to the law, the deceased elder child's wife, who never signed off her right of inheritance, is entitled to the "dowry right" determined by the state of residence. Should she choose to turn a deaf ear to the beseeching of her deceased spouse's younger siblings, she can legally make off with the lion's share of the estate to a new romance and marriage!

But even if the plan goes exactly as diagrammed, the elder son will be subject to federal gift taxes (see chapter 6) if he attempts to pass under-the-table shares of more than eleven thousand dollars to the younger brothers and sisters in any one year. When the government comes to collect its due along with accrued penalties, the younger family members, at least morally obligated to contribute to the fines and penalties, can easily and legally refuse to kick in their share.

---

### Joint Ownership with Minor Children

Be mindful that the one thing worse than entering into joint ownership with children is entering into joint tenancy with *underage* children. This is nothing short of sheer lunacy. Because a minor child cannot inherit on her own, the child's new acquisition automatically brings her under the protection of probate court. A court-appointed conservator will manage the inheritance until the child reaches the age of eighteen.

# UNINTENTIONAL DISINHERITING OF YOUR CHILDREN

Entering joint tenancy with a second husband or wife is one of the best ways known to unintentionally disinherit the children of the first marriage. It is a little-known fact that *joint tenancy always takes precedence over a will or trust.* Because the decedent's share of jointly held property transfers immediately to the surviving joint tenant at the moment of death, there is nothing to transfer later via a will.

Understanding that legality, consider Bob and Betty and their three children. The couple holds all of its assets in joint tenancy and neither spouse has a will. Bob dies and his share of the estate passes immediately to Betty, avoiding probate. Betty, now very aware of her own mortality, draws a will leaving all the property, possessions, and holdings of the marriage to the three children.

Several years later Betty remarries, this time to Jim, a widower with children of his own. Betty and Jim together place all of their assets in joint tenancy, believing such a move will avoid the probate process when they die. A short time later, Betty passes on. Betty and Jim's agreed-to joint tenancy arrangement supersedes Betty's will and the entire estate passes to her second husband, Jim. Because he is now sole owner of *all* the assets, Jim can leave all his property and, if he so chooses, all that of Bob and Betty's to his own children, completely disinheriting Bob and Betty's three children of assets that rightfully should have been theirs.

# JOINT TENANCY IN COMMON

The joint tenancy tales of terror can go on almost to infinity; however, let me tell you that there is also a completely different way to muddy the waters. There are basically two different types of joint tenancy and it is very important to tell them apart should you decide to attempt to ford those waters. Joint Tenancy with Right of Survivorship (often abbreviated to JTWROS) and its previously mentioned cousin,

Tenancy by the Entirety, are very similar. Tenancy by the Entirety differs only in that it must involve a husband and wife and can be terminated only by the mutual consent and joint action of both spouses during their lifetimes.

Joint Tenancy in Common is entirely different, and you should be wary that as you enter into a joint tenancy arrangement you are getting what you ordered from the menu. Joint Tenancy in Common is often used between non-relatives who wish to enter into co-ownership of a boat, hunting lodge, airplane, or some piece of machinery used by all of the tenants. Should one of the co-owners die, his share does not go to the surviving co-owner(s). It instead goes to whomever the decedent names in his will (usually a member of his own family such as a spouse, brother, sister, father, or uncle). That means that assets held in Joint Tenancy in Common must endure probate.

Joint Tenancy in Common, rather than avoiding probate, is a non-stop flight with touchdown on the probate bench runway. Not only is the piece of property tied up in court for months negating the possibility of any sale or possible use of the asset while in probate, it also may eventually place the surviving co-owner(s) in an impossible partnership with people they do not know, or with someone with whom they cannot get along or trust. It is an unusual and difficult form of ownership and one to be avoided if at all possible.

# THE ADVANTAGES AND EVILS OF STEPPED-UP VALUATION

The most cunning joint tenancy trap of all is the one that is least understood and often results in backbreaking capital gains taxes for those who ignorantly become entangled in the ambush. This hidden net is called stepped-up valuation. Regrettably, it is too often explained to clients by accountants and attorneys who presume that their listeners understand all the basics, permitting the attorney or accountant to skip right into the nuts and bolts. Allow me to attempt a more simple explanation.

## Appreciation of Assets

We all hope that our assets will increase in value. We buy stocks in various companies not only expecting those companies to pay us dividends resulting from company profits, but also speculating that our shares will become more valuable and that we will be able to someday sell them for more than what we paid for them. The same is true of a business or home. If our business venture succeeds, when we sell the enterprise we may well make a profit on the assets we invested in it. We don't receive any dividends from our home other than a roof over our heads, but we hope to someday sell our homes for more than we paid for them.

This appreciation in value can be due to several factors. Our assets may become more desirable because of their ability to earn larger profits and dividends or, as in the case of a house or parcel of real estate, because the location becomes more coveted. Also, in the American economy the value of our assets often ascends due to no other determinant than the rate of inflation. Whatever the cause of the appreciation of our assets, the Internal Revenue Service looks upon our good fortune as a *profit* and therefore taxes that profit. It is called capital gains tax. This tax is not due the government until the asset is actually sold and the cash-in-hand profit is realized. This is because should the asset depreciate in value over the period of ownership, as assets occasionally and regrettably do, we would owe the IRS nothing on the sale, and, in fact, would have a capital loss and be able to use that loss as a deduction from our overall income.

## The Capital Gains Trap

The Internal Revenue Service dictates that an asset's value is the equivalent of its market value at the time it was either purchased or inherited. As an example: you purchase a home in 1974 for $50,000. In 2004, thirty years later, the house has a market value of $100,000. However, the IRS says that regardless of its increase in market value, your investment in the home will always remain at $50,000 plus any improvements you made to the home during the time you owned it.

Another example: in 2004 you inherit a house with a market value of $100,000 from your parents at their death. The IRS establishes your investment in the house at its current market value of $100,000, not the $12,000 that your parents paid for the house back in 1949.

Understanding these two rules, follow this scenario to learn how foolish it is to deed appreciating assets, jointly or wholly, to your children before you die:

Frank Jones wants to make sure that the home he purchased in 1973 for $20,000 will go to his son, Jeff, without the need of probate when Frank dies. In 1990, Frank files a quitclaim deed with the county giving Jeff joint ownership in the house. When Frank dies, he figures that his own share of the house will go immediately to his son Jeff through the joint ownership arrangement, without the need for probate.

So now, from an ownership standpoint, the house has been divided into two halves. Frank Jones retains ownership of one half of the house at a reduced investment of $10,000 and his son, Jeff, now owns the other half of the house in joint ownership with his father, also at an investment of $10,000. That all adds up to the original $20,000 Frank Jones paid for the house.

When Frank dies in 2004, inflation has driven the appraised market value of the house to $120,000. Frank's half of the house is inherited by his son, Jeff, at the moment of Frank's death at a value of $60,000, fifty percent of the total value of the 2004 appraisal of the house (remember, after Frank gave half of the house to Jeff back in 1990, Frank then only owned one half of the house).

Note that Jeff can inherit only the half of the house his dad owned when he died; Jeff cannot inherit the other half of the house because he already owns it. It was given to him as a $10,000 gift by his father back in 1990. The Internal Revenue Service now adds Jeff's two halves together (the $60,000 half Jeff received as an inheritance when his father died and the $10,000 half Jeff received as a gift from his father back in 1990) and determines that Jeff's total investment in the house is $70,000.

If Jeff now sells the house for its full 2004 market value of $120,000, we subtract his $70,000 total investment and see that Jeff has realized a profit of $50,000. At current rates (around fifteen

*I'm proud to pay taxes in the United States; the only thing is, I could be just as proud for half the money.*

—ARTHUR GODFREY

percent), Jeff will owe the government approximately $7,500 in capital gains taxes!

Had Frank retained the house fully in his own name until he died (no joint ownership with his son), his son would have inherited the whole house at its full 2004 market value of $120,000. Jeff could have then sold the house for $120,000, tax-free.

---

### Joint Tenancy in Community Property States

It is interesting to note here that in a husband/wife joint ownership, similar to joint tenancy with children, the survivor receives the half owned by the deceased spouse at its new stepped-up value. However, surviving spouses living in community property states (Arizona, California, Idaho, Louisiana, Nevada, New Mexico, Texas, Washington, and Wisconsin) will receive stepped-up valuation on *both* halves.

---

## Wills and Living Trusts

Had Jeff not received half of the house as a gift in 1990 but instead *inherited* the entire house through his father's will in 2004, the probate fees on the house at Frank's death (using the attorney's low estimate of three to six percent) would have probably totaled around $3,600 to $7,200. Surely that is a lot of money, but still significantly cheaper than the $7,500 capital gains taxes due because Frank chose the joint ownership arrangement instead.

Had Frank Jones placed the house in a living trust rather than joint ownership back in 1990, Jeff would have inherited the house through his father's living trust in 2004 and then sold the property at its appraised market value—and there would have been neither capital gains taxes nor probate costs!

Not only has Frank Jones exposed his son to exorbitant capital gains taxes, Frank has exposed himself to all of his son's legal headaches. Jeff is free to mortgage his half of the house (he doesn't need

| ESTIMATED COST TO TRANSFER HOME TO HEIRS | | | |
|---|---|---|---|
| Current Value of Home: $120,000 Purchase Price of Home 30 Years Ago: $20,000 | | | |
| | **Will** | **Joint Tenancy** | **Living Trust** |
| Estimated court costs | $2,400 | 0 | 0 |
| Estimated attorney fee* | $3,600 | 0 | 0 |
| Capital gains tax | 0 | $7,500 | 0 |
| **Total Cost** | $6,000 | $7,500 | $0 |

\* Based on the low 3% fee quoted by the legal profession.

his father's permission) and Jeff's creditors will have the right to place a lien on the house; a house that once-upon-a-time belonged one hundred percent to Frank Jones, free and clear.

Clearly, joint ownership is the most expensive way of all to convey assets to your children!

## Capital Gains Tax Exemptions

The old once-in-a-lifetime capital gains tax exemption of $125,000 available to those over the age of fifty-five has been dumped in favor of a $250,000 exemption ($500,000 when assets are joint ownership) that can be used once every two years with no age restriction. However, this so-called windfall exemption bump is of very little value to an heir or beneficiary. The hitch is that the resident must have lived in the house for twenty-four of the last sixty months to claim the exemption. Thus, a house not considered to be a homestead is not eligible for the exemption.

For Jeff to qualify for this exemption he would have to move out of his own home and into his father's home for a period of two years.

After his father's death, upon selling his father's home, Jeff would then not be eligible for another exemption for an additional two years. He must wait two years after his father's death before he could entertain any profitable offer from a buyer to purchase his *own* home without giving the government fifteen percent of his good fortune in capital gains taxes.

---

### Keeping up with Capital Gains Taxes

In choosing the best technique for transferring your property, it's important to consider current capital gains tax rates. It is possible that between exorbitant attorney fees and unavoidable court costs, the expense of probate could exceed what you would pay in capital gains taxes. However, this tax is just one of many pitfalls of joint tenancy. And remember, both probate fees and capital gains taxes are easily avoided with a living trust.

---

## JOINT OWNERSHIP IS A LANDMINE

Joint Tenancy with Right of Survivorship is loaded with booby traps. At best it succeeds only in the deferral of the probate process while at the same time reducing control over assets and exposing the original owners to liability, lawsuits, and unintentional disinheriting of children, and exposing heirs to unexpected backbreaking capital gains tax assessments.

Joint tenancy is usually suggested to the wife by a devoted, but uninformed husband altruistically thinking of his wife's welfare after he is gone. However, from the outset there is a fifty-fifty chance of a backfire. What if the wife dies first? The property all reverts to the husband's sole ownership and he is right back to square one and faced once again with the problem of avoiding probate and the conservation of his assets for the use of his children after he dies.

The joint tenancy solution has always been very popular among the pseudo experts that hold court daily in the barbershops and bowling alleys of the nation. These self-appointed estate-planning authorities know little about the hidden taxes involved, lack of stepped-up valuation, and loss of asset control. Indeed, most of the estate planning errors such as joint ownership with a spouse or with children can be attributed to advice received from unqualified amateurs, bystanders, and the wisenheimer neighbor next door. The rest of it comes from attorneys who selfishly want to keep their clients out of a living trust for the purpose of initiating an expensive probate of the entire estate after the surviving spouse has died.

As I said at the beginning of this chapter, joint tenancy of assets is truly fool's gold and any advice that advocates joint tenancy as an estate-planning alternative should be taken with several grains of salt.

# 4

# So What the Heck Is a Living Trust?

There is only one way to get assets out of your name, maintain complete control of them, and protect your children from exorbitant capital gains taxes. It's called a living trust.

A living trust is officially called a revocable *inter vivos* trust, a Latin mouthful ranking right up there with such legalese as *fieri facias, habeas corpus*, and *caveat emptor* and often used to scare the amateur right into the waiting arms of an attorney. The term *inter vivos* means "created while alive" (as if you could create something after you are dead). However, rather than being indicative of one's mortality at the moment of the trust's creation, the more popular moniker "living trust" better describes the options of this estate-planning tool in contrast to a will.

## WHY LIVING TRUSTS ARE LEGAL

Just like probate, the concept of the trust has been with us for centuries, and, for the most part, has erroneously been associated with the very wealthy as a means of minimizing income taxes. However, there are many different trusts, which accomplish very different functions.

A trust operates quite similarly to a corporation. Attorneys are often anxious to head off prospective clients' interests in a living trust and divert them to the more lucrative probate process via a Last Will and Testament. Thus, they often resort to an old prevarication that trusts are nothing more than loopholes in our tax structure that ultimately will be closed, thereby rendering any trust made by the client illegal. What nonsense!

The right of all American citizens to do business as a corporation or under an assumed name or as a fictitious person (trust) has been with us for centuries. The trust has been recognized in law for nearly five hundred years, having been ruled legal in Chancery Court of England in A.D. 1535. Your right to create a living trust in the United States is indirectly guaranteed by the Tenth Amendment to the United States Constitution, which leaves certain rights and privileges to the individual states. Such intervention by the federal government into the personal rights of the citizenry would quickly bring chaos to the entire financial composition of the nation. Every corporation in the country, large or small (including each of those listed in the stock market report of today's newspaper), would be unable to conduct business. The Maple Grove Motel, Village Square Bakery, and thousands upon thousands of privately owned, small businesses operating under an assumed name would all have to change their commercial label to that of the proprietor or go out of business. There is no more danger of the government attempting to outlaw trusts than there is of the government trying to outlaw General Motors, General Electric, or Grandma Ginny's General Store.

## THE TWO CATEGORIES OF TRUSTS

Though there are many variations, trusts generally can be categorized into two basic types.

## Irrevocable Trusts

The basic *irrevocable trust,* once made, cannot be canceled or altered by anyone, including its creator. The creator of the trust sets aside certain property or funds for the current or future use of someone else. The creator of such a trust must relinquish all rights to those assets forever and appoints a *trustee* to manage the assets and later distribute those assets to the person(s) named as beneficiaries by the trust creator. Irrevocable trusts are unchangeable, and the creator of the trust loses all personal control of those assets and forfeits the privilege of changing any provision of the trust or receiving any income from it. As they say, "it is written in granite."

So what's the advantage of an irrevocable trust? Because the creator of an irrevocable trust can no longer receive any profits or benefits from those trust-held assets or, for that matter, even get his assets back, the creator of such a trust no longer has to pay income taxes on the earnings from those assets. And because in most cases the creator of the trust was going to will those assets to the very people named as beneficiaries, it makes more sense to officially earmark those assets before death and allow the beneficiaries (often in a lower tax bracket) to have the earnings from them ahead of time.

## Revocable Trusts

It is important to understand that the living trust belongs in the second of the two basic types of trusts. The *revocable trust* allows any provision or beneficiary to be changed or canceled at any time by its creator. This type of trust has grown rapidly in popularity in this country during the last four decades and bears little resemblance to the irrevocable and sometimes disreputable trusts of the 1920s.

The difference of course is in the key words "irrevocable" and "revocable." The irrevocable trusts of earlier years were a tradeoff; they swapped control of a portion of one's wealth for a healthy income tax dodge.

In contrast, the creator of the revocable living trust makes no regulatory sacrifices. The living trust remains under the complete control of its founder at all times, even to the extent of being able to completely void the entire trust if the creator so chooses.

Having the power to alter or cancel the trust eliminates the income tax shelter characteristic; however, the revocable living trust becomes

**Testamentary Trusts**

You should also be aware that in addition to an *inter vivos* trust, there also exists what is known as a *testamentary* trust. A testamentary trust is created by the terms in a Last Will and Testament, which means testamentary trusts are set up after death. The attorney falsely tells an unenlightened client that he will lose control of his assets if he places them in a trust before he dies. The attorney then designs the documents for both a will and a trust; however, the assets are intentionally not transferred into the name of trust and must undergo the full trappings of probate. When probate is completed, twelve to twenty-four months after death, the probate judge places the assets in the trust. A trustee appointed in the trust contract then distributes the assets from the testamentary trust to the beneficiaries, usually within just a few hours, which renders the whole procedure a complete waste of time and money—except of course to the attorney. The attorney collects a double fee by charging the client to probate the estate and at the same time charging the client to create a trust. The attorney has accomplished the feat of soaking the client twice.

instead an uncomplicated and viable alternative to the evils of joint tenancy and the expense and headaches of probating an estate. At the same time it offers the very real possibility of a great deal of savings on estate and capital gains taxes. It is within the safe harbor of revocable trusts that the rapidly growing popularity of the living trust is anchored.

## ABCs OF A LIVING TRUST

Understand, first of all, that a living trust is not a piece of paper. Regardless of what some attorney or associate has told you, a living trust is not some trick document that you can sign and make all of your estate-planning problems go away. Instead, a living trust is one of the four methods or techniques of owning and/or controlling private assets. You are already familiar with three of those techniques. You choose the one you want by the manner in which you name the owner(s) on the title or deed of an asset.

## The Four Techniques of Asset Ownership

1. SOLE OWNERSHIP:   Your name and no one else's appears on the title, deed, or account as the owner of the asset. That means that you alone own the asset.

2. JOINT TENANCY (OR JOINT OWNERSHIP) WITH RIGHT OF SURVIVORSHIP:   Two or more people own an asset in equal shares (see Chapter 3). The names of each person owning a share appear on the title or deed of the asset or the bank account in which the asset is held. Joint Tenancy with Right of Survivorship (JTWROS) is used almost universally by married couples.

3. CORPORATION:   An asset is owned by two or more people in equal or unequal shares. Each owner is issued a title called a "stock certificate" that indicates what portion of the corporation's total assets she owns.

   The problem is that with all three of the above techniques of ownership, you must own the asset to control the asset. If you sell the asset or give it to another person you lose control of it. Any under-the-table written or verbal agreement as to whom the new owner must bequeath the assets at his death would have no legal merit in court. Thus, all three of these ownership methods are very poor estate-planning techniques. Each leads directly to probate court.

   Very few people are familiar with the fourth technique of ownership:

4. TRUST:   Assets held in trust ownership avoid probate and, when not messed up with a lot of needless legalese, the expensive services of an attorney at death. You create a trust by instructing your financial custodians (bank, stockbroker, credit union, etc.) to replace the original title, deed, or account to the asset with a new title that

designates the asset is owned by your trust rather than by you. Your name still appears on the title, but now as the *trustee* rather than as the owner.

## The Common Link of All Fictitious Entities

A trust is a fictitious entity, and very similar to a corporation or municipality. The Ford Motor Company is a fictitious entity. Chicago is a fictitious entity. Charlie McCarthy, the smart-mouthed, wooden dummy of ventriloquist Edgar Bergen of half a century ago was a fictitious entity. Fictitious entities can have an identity and a personality, even a spot on a map if they are a municipality, but they are not real, live persons.

However, just as the city, village, or township in which you live owns buildings, trucks, snowplows, and bank accounts, a trust can own assets in its own name. Perhaps the most difficult element of a living trust for some people to understand is the fact that an asset can be owned by something other than a real, live human being. That is the key to the success of a living trust. Those that cannot grasp this concept will probably never completely understand a living trust.

Trusts have one thing in common with corporations, municipalities, puppets, and other fictitious entities: they are dumber than a box of rocks. They can't talk, they can't walk, they can't think, and they can't reason or do any of the other things that a human being can do. A fictitious entity requires a board of directors, a mayor, or a ventriloquist to make decisions for it and guide its destiny. The manager of the fictitious person known as a trust is called the *trustee*.

## Maintaining Control of Your Assets

As the maker of your trust, you will draw a simple written agreement with the trustee or manager of your trust to assure that he will manage the trust according to your wishes.

But how do you maintain control over assets you no longer own? You appoint yourself and, if you are married, your spouse as the trustees of the trust! That means that as the grantor (maker) of the trust you get to write rules that allow you, as the trustee of the trust, to do as you please with the trust assets—even though those assets now belong to the trust rather than you. And because the trust is revocable, you (as the grantor) can write additional rules at a later date that will allow you (as the trustee) to take care of any future detail that you did not foresee when you first drew the trust contract.

## The Undying Living Trust

Though the makers of the trust—you and your spouse—will eventually die, the legal owner of the assets—the trust—will remain very much alive. A *successor trustee* appointed in the trust contract by you while you are alive will step in at your death and become the new trustee. This person is usually one or all of your adult children, some other close relative, or your most devoted friend.

It would be the same thing if the president of the Kellogg Company in Battle Creek, Michigan, died tomorrow morning at breakfast. By lunchtime a vice-president would have assumed the presidency and Kellogg's would go right on churning out Rice Krispies cereal. A trust works exactly the same way.

The successor trustee has no authority whatsoever while you and your spouse are alive, but at your deaths assumes full power to do as the terms of the trust contract dictate (pay the bills and taxes, then distribute the remainder of the assets to the beneficiaries). The successor trustee cannot, however, change any of the trust's terms any more than the new president of the Kellogg Company could change rules set down by Kellogg's stockholders through the board of directors.

If the affairs of the trust are in good order, this distribution of the assets to the beneficiaries at your death will take perhaps three to ten days and the cost of transfer will probably be less than fifty dollars. This cost is incurred entirely by the out-of-pocket expenses of the successor trustee(s). Such items as a quitclaim deed to transfer real estate on to the beneficiaries, phone calls, postage, stationery, and a tank of gas in the successor trustee's Chevy are legitimate expenses that the trust should rightly pick up.

## COST COMPARISON: LIVING TRUSTS VS. A WILL

### $150,000 ESTATE

| Living Trust | | Last Will and Testament | |
|---|---|---|---|
| Estimated cost to create the trust | $500 | Estimated cost to write will | $250 |
| Estimated cost to transfer assets | $50 | Probate costs: | |
| | | estimated lawyer's fees* | $4,500 |
| | | estimated court costs | $3,000 |
| Estimated cost for family to terminate trust at death | $50 | Estimated personal representative's fee | $2,250 |
| TOTAL ESTIMATED COSTS | $600 | TOTAL ESTIMATED COSTS | $10,000 |

### $750,000 ESTATE

| Living Trust | | Last Will and Testament | |
|---|---|---|---|
| Estimated cost to create the trust | $500 | Estimated cost to write will | $250 |
| Estimated cost to transfer assets | $50 | Probate costs: | |
| | | estimated lawyer's fees* | $22,500 |
| | | estimated court costs | $15,000 |
| Estimated cost for family to terminate trust at death | $50 | Estimated personal representative's fee | $11,250 |
| TOTAL ESTIMATED COSTS | $600 | TOTAL ESTIMATED COSTS | $49,000 |

*Based on the low 3% fee quoted by the legal profession. The actual percentage is usually higher.

Best of all, your beneficiaries will receive the assets from your trust at their full, stepped-up value at the time of your death. Your beneficiaries may then sell those assets at their present market value without incurring any capital gains taxes.

## CREATING A TRUST IS A FIFTEEN-MINUTE PROCESS

Transferring assets into the trust is simple and easy. It takes fifteen minutes or less to transfer an asset into a trust. This of course does not include the time spent cooling your heels in the lobby waiting your turn or engaging the banker in small talk concerning today's weather.

It matters not that the asset may be mortgaged. There is really little need even to inform the lender that you have transferred the property from private ownership to trust ownership. The lender is protected by 1) your signature on the mortgage and 2) your pledge of the asset as collateral. It matters little to the lender in which technique you choose to title the asset. If you personally do not continue to make the payments, the lender will come and get the house as prescribed in the mortgage, regardless of the technique of ownership in which the asset is titled.

To help justify their $1,500 to $3,000 fees for drawing trust documents, many attorneys attempt to convey the idea that the transfer of assets into the trust is a time-consuming and difficult procedure that will require the attorney's assistance. Don't believe it!

The same procedure used to open a checking account is used to transfer assets to a trust. Therefore, you don't need an attorney to transfer assets to a trust any more than you needed an attorney to assist you in opening your checking account. Your financial custodians will be happy to make the change for you. You need only request it. A single, memorized statement will set the whole process in motion. Simply exhibit your signed trust contract and say to your banker or other financial custodian:

"I would like to open a new account today. It will be in the name of my new living trust."

| BASIC ELEMENTS OF A LIVING TRUST VS. A WILL | |
| --- | --- |
| **Living Trust** | **Last Will and Testament** |
| ▶ Names grantors of the trust | ▶ Names the testator |
| ▶ Names the primary trustees of the trust; sets down the rules and regulations by which trustees must manage the trust and trust assets | ▶ Does not become active until after the testator's death |
| ▶ Names a successor trustee who will take over the management of the trust upon the death of the primary trustee | ▶ Names a personal representative to locate assets, creditors, and debtors of the deceased testator |
| ▶ Names the beneficiaries who will receive the assets after the trust grantor is dead | ▶ Names heirs to receive assets after all debts, legal fees, and taxes have been paid |
| ▶ Not subject to attorney fees or court costs associated with probate (except in the case of assets held outside of the trust) | ▶ Subject to attorney fees and court costs associated with probate |
| ▶ Private contract between grantor and trustee, to which only the custodians of the grantor's assets are privy | ▶ All probate records and hearings are open to the public |
| ▶ Can be challenged in Civil Court | ▶ Can be challenged in Probate Court |
| ▶ Personal guardian for underage children named in separate auxiliary document (subject to court's approval) | ▶ Names a personal guardian to physically rear any underage children of the deceased (subject to court's approval) |
| ▶ Underage children's assets managed by successor trustee, often through a children's trust | ▶ Names a property guardian to manage the assets of any underage children (subject to court's approval) |

That's all it takes! At that point your financial custodian will pick up the ball and run with it while you sit there and watch. All you are doing is opening a new account, transferring your assets from your old account to your new account, and then closing your old account. In effect, you are simply taking the money out of one pocket and putting it in another.

The financial custodian will quickly complete all the paperwork and the only thing you will be required to do is sign your name two or three times in the spaces provided. There are no secret handshakes. The financial custodian probably goes through the same procedure for two or three customers every day of the week.

Real estate is transferred into the trust with a quitclaim deed that you can pick up at almost any office supply store and then fill out on your dining room table in ten minutes using information off your present deed or a tax notice. You will then have the quitclaim deed recorded at the county registrar of deeds office in or near the courthouse.

In so many words the quitclaim deed will say, "for a consideration of less than $100, John and Jane Doe convey the property described herein to the Doe Family Trust, John and Jane Doe, Trustees."

Again, pretty simple, huh?

## THE SIMPLE REQUIREMENTS OF A LIVING TRUST CONTRACT

You will need to show your financial custodian two or three pages from your trust contract before the financial custodian can transfer your assets to the trust. The two requirements of your trust contract are:

1. the naming of a trustee (or manager) to manage the trust
2. the naming of a successor trustee to take over the management of the trust when the original trustee (you) is dead

Nothing else is required to make a legal trust contract. Two hundred–page, leather-bound trust contracts drawn by attorneys almost always contain pointless financial details, useless asset descriptions, and needless legalese to deliberately confuse the successor trustee and drive him back into the arms of the attorney to unscramble the trust and settle the estate upon death. In such cases the attorney's fee for fabricating this unnecessary service of wrapping up the trust often rivals what the attorney would have charged to probate the estate.

Because more than a few folks judge a package by its size and its pretty wrappings, rather than its content, many attorneys pad the trust package with needless affidavits, abstracts, letters of intent, indices, tables of content, and lots and lots of legalese. Such nonessential "stuffing," turned out by the attorney's secretary on a computer in seconds for a few cents extra cost, serves to thicken the packet of trust documents and visually justify the price the attorney must charge to cover her office overhead and profit margin.

### Less Is More

Invariably, the simpler the trust contract, the better the trust you have. Superfluous trust packages require frequent amending each time you change any one of the needless details or buy, sell, or trade an asset. Attorney fees to write such amendments generally range from $150 to $500, depending on the complexity of the amendment. This make-work philosophy is considered entirely ethical by the legal profession.

It is also important to understand that trust assets are identified by what is written in the titles and deeds of the assets, not what is written in the trust contract. There is absolutely no need for a properly constructed trust contract to formally list the assets owned by the trust. A simple paragraph in the trust contract states that any asset whose title bears as its owner the name of the trust and its trustees does away with the need to list the assets of the trust in the trust contract. It is, however, a courtesy to the successor trustee to place with the trust documents an informal list that not only identifies the trust's assets but also the location of the title or deed of each asset.

Listing the assets directly in the trust contract has absolutely no legal merit whatsoever and serves only to:

- needlessly add to the length of the contract for which the attorney can charge

- reveal to your attorney your approximate net worth, which gives the attorney a guide as to what she thinks you can afford

You prove that you have complied with the two requirements of naming a trustee and a successor trustee simply by showing the trust contract to your financial custodians. It does not matter if an attorney has drawn the contract or if you have done it for yourself. In fact, the identity of the person or law firm that wrote the contract is none of the financial custodian's business. If your financial custodians are satisfied that your trust contract contains these two basic elements listed above, they should be able to transfer the assets out of your name and into the name of your trust in fifteen minutes or less.

# 5

## The Legal Side: Conceptions and Misconceptions

**N**o attorney in her right mind wants her clients to know what it is that makes a trust legal. (The attorney might not know herself.) To learn what makes a trust legal would open the eyes of the client to the realization that the client did not need the attorney in the first place.

### THE ULTIMATE GOAL OF A LIVING TRUST

To understand the legalities of a living trust you must have a firm grip on two factors:

- what your trust is attempting to accomplish

- the long-standing fiduciary laws by which all financial custodians must abide

To say that your trust is attempting to accomplish the "avoidance of probate" is not enough. You are really trying to convince your financial custodians that they can safely release your assets to your heirs after you die, free from the fear of lawsuit by dissatisfied heirs, without the need of a guarantee from probate court. That is the name of the game!

Let's consider for a moment your assets as you presently hold them in sole ownership, joint ownership, and corporations.

The moment your financial custodians accepted your assets for safekeeping in these privately held accounts, they obligated themselves to return those assets to you upon your demand. This obligation did not come about out of the goodness of their hearts. They would much rather continue to borrow money from you via your deposits at two to two and one-half percent and then loan the money back to you at nine percent. (Their stockholders consider this to be a great way for them to get rich.) Instead, that obligation to return your money upon demand came about from inflexible fiduciary laws that have guarded the hard-earned savings of the public for centuries.

No one suddenly decides to become a banker or stockbroker and then hangs out a shingle that says "Open for Business." Though they are privately owned, banks, credit unions, and stockbrokers are chartered by the federal or state government and must agree to certain regulations such as guarding your assets to the best of their ability and returning your assets to you the moment you make that request, no questions asked.

Because of this legal obligation to return your privately held assets upon demand, the legality of any account in which money is to be held must be determined when the account is opened and funds deposited or invested, not at the time the funds are withdrawn. When you open a new savings account you must first fill out an application and answer a few simple questions. When you want the money back, simply fill out a withdrawal slip, take it to the teller and say, "give me my money." You don't even have to say "please" if you don't want to.

## APPLYING COMMON SENSE

Now, comes the moment of truth attorneys would rather you not understand. This fiduciary obligation of the financial custodian to return your assets upon demand is not diminished by the fact that the asset is owned by a trust. The financial custodian is legally bound to return the asset to the trustee of the trust the moment the trustee asks that it be returned. To refuse to release the asset to the trustee would be tantamount to your bank denying you access to the funds you currently hold privately in that bank. The banking commission would have them shut down and put out of business within days.

Hence, no court, no attorney, nor any judge has anything to say about the legality of your trust. The magic moment when your trust becomes legal is that instant when the financial custodian completes the examination of your trust contract and accepts your assets for safekeeping in an account owned by your trust. The acceptance of your trust-owned assets by your financial custodian guarantees that those assets must be released to the control of your successor trustee immediately upon your death.

Again, what is it that you set out to accomplish? Without resorting to expensive probate court, you wished to remove your financial custodian's fear of lawsuits from disgruntled and disinherited heirs, thus permitting that financial custodian to release your assets directly and immediately to your appointed heirs.

This is finally accomplished when the successor trustee, using the authority given him through the bylaws of the trust contract, simply turns around and gives those assets to the beneficiaries named by the trust grantor(s) in the trust contract, thereby terminating the trust.

What this all means is that an attorney has absolutely nothing to sell you other than a simple contract between you and your trustee—you and you! (How complex must that document be to keep you from cheating yourself?) It also means that any intimidating threats made by an attorney that you will get in terrible trouble by not employing him to establish the trust are baseless and nothing more than a thinly veiled attempt to line his own pockets.

Whether you pay $395 or $2,395 for your trust documents, there is no such thing as an illegal living trust.

## CONTRASTS IN PHILOSOPHY

All things considered, it is the philosophical differences between the living trust and the probate system that are the most difficult for living trust neophytes to grasp.

## The Philosophy of Probate

Probate is a very public and complex affair requiring the expensive services of a professional to unscramble. Your Last Will and Testament is nothing more than a wish list and an automatic summons to this public hearing presided over by the state in which you live through its local arm called county probate court.

Both the will and the probate proceedings are open books that will not only be officially and legally scrutinized by the judge, attorney, and various other officers of the court, but also by creditors, relatives, friends, neighbors, enemies, and anyone else who thinks she might be able to manipulate the decedent's wishes enough to get an extra dime out of the settlement. Every "T" must be crossed and every comma must have a tail. The survivors of the decedent have no alternative but to sit helplessly by, waiting for the world to finish sifting through the private financial affairs of the family.

A person who chooses to divide his estate among his heirs using the technique of a Last Will and Testament has only the word of the attorney that drew the will that the instrument is without error. It is the probate judge, perhaps years later, who officially examines the will after the testator has died and rules on its validity. Should the judge find unresolvable errors, he may throw the will out of court and rule that the decedent died intestate, a decision that can create a king-sized headache for the decedent's family.

# The Philosophy of the Living Trust

Lecturing attorneys and estate planners harangue long and loud about the dangers of clients circumventing their unrealistic professional fees to instead either draw their own trusts or purchase a commercial living trust kit. Thus, it is of extreme importance for students of the living trust strategy to realize that the living trust is unique among all legal procedures. Unlike the conflicts involved in getting divorced, filing for bankruptcy, suing someone for default on an agreement, battling for the custody of a child, evicting a deadbeat tenant, or purchasing a $200,000 house from a stranger, it is difficult in the trust-making business to find an adversary.

The custodians of the assets certainly are not going to give the trust maker any problems. The trust maker is a customer of the financial custodian. Financial custodians make money only when their customers are happy with the custodian's services. They will register your assets in the name of Mickey Mouse if you say so.

A grantor setting up a trust in which she acts as trustee certainly does not need to be protected from herself. And in reality, a corporate trustee (bank, investment house, or trust company) is an employee. To put an end to any altercation, the grantor need only amend the trust, fire the trustee, and replace it with someone else.

There is only one possible person that might usurp the grantor's wishes or expropriate the assets: the *successor trustee* who assumes control of the trust affairs after the original trustee (the grantor) is dead. Therefore, let's put the successor trustee's role through the wringer.

First of all, it must be remembered that the grantor has a binding contract with the trustee. When the successor trustee replaces the primary trustee (you), that successor trustee assumes the obligations of the contract. Even with the grantors dead, the contract and its terms can be enforced in the courts by the beneficiaries.

However, successor trustees are rarely selected because they are easily frightened with the caveat of ten years in prison. Instead, they are selected for their character, integrity, fidelity, and the fact that their interests and goals are in complete harmony with those of the grantor.

The choice of successor trustee is easily the most important decision the grantor will make in the organization of her trust—ten times as significant as the grantor's choice of an attorney or executor. It is this backup trustee that does the heavy lifting of settling the trust. That successor trustee is almost always one or all of the grantor's adult children, some other close relative, or the grantor's most devoted friend. The successor trustee has an established interest in doing everything possible to expediently carry out the grantor's wishes.

Why?

Because in almost every case, the successor trustee is also one of the beneficiaries. He has a very covetous incentive: he is anxious to cash his own inheritance check.

The legal profession would like you to believe that drawing your own trust document, having it drawn privately, or purchasing one of the living trust kits on the market is akin to playing with matches in a gun powder factory; that one minute error in your trust document will throw your entire estate into utter chaos. This is a scare tactic and simply not true. Among those who know better, such a ploy succeeds only in casting shame on the integrity of the legal profession.

A nitpicking probate judge can completely destroy a carelessly written will while the attorney and family look on helplessly. However, unless they are invited, no court, no judge, no attorney, no policeman has any jurisdiction in the settlement of a living trust. There is but a paltry chance that any legal entity other than the notary public that witnesses your signature will ever set eyes on your living trust document.

> *My daddy is a movie actor and sometimes he plays the good guy and sometimes he plays the lawyer.*
>
> —HARRISON FORD'S SON

## Self-Regulation

The entire living trust approach is a self-regulated system. It is a private contract made between a grantor and a trustee (usually one and the same person) to which only the custodians of the grantor's assets are privy. There are no public notices, no open hearings at the courthouse, no attorneys or dyspeptic judges who believe the widow is not shedding enough tears, no creditors waving five-year-old dunning notices,

no nosy neighbors, and no greedy relatives. It is no one's business other than that of the immediate family.

Your successor trustee is on his own and has sovereign control. After taxes have been determined and bills paid, he has the authority simply to overlook minor flaws in the trust document and get on with the settlement of the trust and the distribution of the assets just as the grantor of the trust directed. This singular ideological difference between the living trust and probate system of settling an estate is always the most difficult for living trust apprentices to perceive.

The mindset nurtured by civilized society that all human entitlement springs from some governmental agency is deeply entrenched. However, in a free land, government has no authority to give; it can only take away. One may argue that government is the source of welfare and many types of grants, but in reality it is the citizens themselves who are the money source. The only funds the government has to "give" come from the taxes it has "taken" away from the citizens. Consequently, in an era where the tentacles of government envelop us from every direction, it is often difficult to maintain the realization that in the course of human events, most activities require no license or permission. Beyond the government's responsibility to protect the financial custodians of a decedent, the affairs of the decedent remain outside the reach of government. Remove the financial custodian's need of shelter from litigation and no government entity or court has any jurisdiction whatsoever in the passing of assets from one generation to the next.

If yours is to be a simple probate-avoiding living trust and you are vacillating between 1) drawing your own documents, 2) having them done privately, or 3) having it done for you by an attorney out of fear that unseen legal gremlins are awaiting the opportunity to sabotage the settlement of your estate, you well may be able to resolve the dilemma by asking yourself the following question:

*Are my family and personal relationships such that I require thousands of dollars' worth of professional legal work to protect me from the most trusted people in my life?*

If your answer to the above question is yes, then you have no business even considering a living trust. You should stick with the probate system where you will have an attorney to run interference for you on every play; you are going to need it. The key word in a living trust is *trust*. The key ingredient in a living trust is a *loving and trustworthy family.* If you are blessed with that, I promise that everything else will fall in place.

## CHALLENGING A LIVING TRUST

Unlike a Last Will and Testament, which can usually be contested sans attorney in probate court by paying a filing fee of perhaps fifteen dollars, it is an extreme rarity that a living trust is ever legally challenged, and even more unusual when one is actually overturned. This is mostly because the living trust is settled with such agility and speed that overlooked relatives (should there be any) simply do not have enough time, the necessary data, or the legal grounds to retard the final resolution of the trust.

A living trust is a civil matter over which probate court has no jurisdiction. Disappointed kindred must grind their axes months later in civil court against each separate beneficiary rather than being allowed the much easier and inexpensive luxury of arguing directly against the estate in probate court.

Litigation in civil court is an entirely different ball game and in such circumstances is an extremely complicated, expensive, and high-risk venture that few attorneys operating on contingency fees want to take. Only the most obstinate grumbler with an exceedingly large burr under his tail will risk his own funds in an attempt to storm the courthouse from such an out-gunned position.

Understand also that, unlike a will, your trust is a private contract between two consenting parties: the grantor and the trustee. Private contracts are unchallengeable unless they violate someone's civil rights or ask one of the parties to commit an illegal act in carrying out the terms of the contract.

The malcontent has only two presentable grounds. First she can say that the grantor of the trust was under duress at the time the trust was drawn. That is, someone had a gun to the head of the grantor and was influential in the terms of the trust. Such cases are very difficult to prove in civil court.

Second, the argument can be used that the grantor was mentally incompetent at the time the trust contract was drawn. This thesis is also very difficult to prove. Unlike a will that has no power until its maker is actually dead, a trust is a working document almost from its inception. All kinds of people and business firms have been doing business with the trust for several years. It will be difficult in a court of law to compel respected bankers, investment brokers, credit union employees, and government officials to admit they have been duped into dealing with an incompetent person all these years.

But in the end it comes back to money—the complainant's money. When it comes to challenging a living trust, no one knows better than the attorneys that the odds of winning such a case in civil court are infinitesimal. Once the attorney explains these things to the complainer along with the fact that his fee is three hundred dollars per hour and the meter is running, the grumbler usually puts on his hat, says to the attorney "I'll have to think about it," and heads for home.

In the comfortable surroundings of the would-be combatant's own living room, reality sets in. After some rational thought, complainers in almost every case decide they have very little to gain and a great deal to lose, and that it makes little sense to walk into a civil lawsuit with the other side holding all the cards.

> *"No man's life, liberty, or property are safe while the legislature is in session."*
>
> —Judge Gideon J. Tucker

# 6

# The Tax Man Cometh— and Taketh

A living trust does not affect local taxes. It won't change the valuation of your home nor alter your homestead exemption in any way. Neither is there an effect on your income taxes. In fact, while both spouses are alive, no federal income tax return is even required for your living trust.

Your income is reported on your standard IRS 1040 form just as you have been reporting it for years. Uncle Sam says that you are the primary beneficiary of a revocable trust and entitled to every cent the trust makes while you are alive. The government wants you to report that income as your personal income just as if no trust existed. Your income taxes will come out to the very same amount—trust or no trust.

We have already discussed in Chapter 3 the capital gains tax problems associated with giving assets to your children, jointly or wholly, before death, as well as the relief a living trust can offer this situation. It is, however, in the land of federal estate taxes where the living trust really shines.

## TAX EXEMPTION INCREASES

Because of the increase in exemptions in recent years you should first know that federal taxes on estates have ceased to be the overwhelming problem they once were. Yet there remains a great deal of confusion concerning estate taxes. Estate taxes have nothing to do with the cost of probate or capital gains taxes. They are three different thieves, each trying to steal your money. Federal estate taxes are assessed on the net value (after debts and encumbrances are considered) of the assets that you transfer to your heirs when you die. The possibility of estate taxes being due is present regardless of the technique in which you title your assets, whether it's sole ownership, joint ownership, corporation, or trust. (Note also that certain states levy state inheritance taxes. However, because those taxes vary so widely from state to state—and many are gradually abolishing this tax altogether—state inheritance taxes are not discussed in this book. See pages 205–207 for a listing of official federal and state tax office Web sites.)

## Common Misconceptions

For almost two decades each person was allowed a $600,000 exemption on the total inheritances he passed to his heirs. A heavy tax of thirty-seven percent kicked in on any excess over $600,000 and graduated up to fifty-five percent when the excess hit $3 million. In other words, a husband and wife each had a $600,000 exemption and, by using their individual exemptions wisely, could pass a total of up to $1.2 million to their children without any estate taxes.

In the course of those twenty years, the $600,000 figure became the basis for many false rumors and fallacies. As an example: many folks still believe (with the assistance of the legal profession's prevarications) $600,000 to be the level at which the probate process begins—and that estates of a lesser amount do not require probate. This is totally untrue. Once again, probate and estate taxes are different beasts, each trying to gobble up a portion of your estate.

---

### Beware of the World Wide Web

To add to the bewilderment, the Internet shamefully hosts hundreds of tax-related Web sites that were abandoned years ago by their makers. Yet the makers of the sites never bothered to take them offline. Hence, instead of spreading enlightenment, these Web sites disseminate nothing more than out-of-date tax information to innocent and unsuspecting visitors. (Official federal and state tax sites are listed on pages 205–207.)

---

## Into the Sunset

Let us get back to the exemptions. The $600,000 federal estate exemption was increased to $625,000 per person on January 1, 1998, increased again to $650,000 on January 1, 1999, and then to $675,000 on January 1, 2000.

The exemption was scheduled to continue to rise almost every year until it reached $1 million per person in the year 2006. However, in

May of 2001, after a long and bitter political struggle in Washington D.C., all of this came to an end and newer, more liberal exemptions were substituted.

The federal estate tax exemption schedule is now set as follows:

| ESTATE TAX EXEMPTIONS THROUGH 2010 |
| --- |
| **January 1, 2004** . . . . . . . . . . . . . . . . . . . . . $1,500,000 per person |
| **January 1, 2006** . . . . . . . . . . . . . . . . . . . . . $2,000,000 per person |
| **January 1, 2009** . . . . . . . . . . . . . . . . . . . . . $3,500,000 per person |
| **January 1, 2010** . . . . . . . . . . . . . . . . . . . . . federal estate taxes discontinued |

If the net value of your estate exceeds this schedule, at death you will owe the government an estate tax starting at thirty-nine percent on the excess over the exemption and sliding upwards to an eventual maximum forty-five percent. Note that the maximum amount reduces from the 2001 level of fifty-five percent to forty-five percent over the eight-year period.

The federal estate tax is scheduled to phase completely out in the year 2010. On the surface all of this appears to be good news until one looks ahead fifty-two more weeks to see what happens January 1, 2011. Congress passed a tax bill under "budget rules" which require an expiration or "sunset" date of 2010 when this temporary law must be repealed. Unless Congress acts to make these tax cuts permanent by 2010 or earlier, the federal estate tax will automatically renew January 1, 2011, with the exemption placed at $1 million per person and the maximum tax on the excess back to fifty-five percent.

Much is still unclear because of the possibility of changes in the capital gains tax structure scheduled for adjustment in the same year (2010) that may make for some tough sledding for estate taxes. Also, the United States Constitution mandates five congressional elections and at least one and possibly two administration changes through the year 2010. This will create a horde of new political candidates pulling and pandering in ways that we at this time cannot imagine.

The new exemption schedule has rewarded the big bucks contributors who keep the legislators in office with a huge windfall. Also, lots of profitable estate-planning work has been manufactured for the legislators' fellow attorneys back home because many trusts and wills must be adjusted to take advantage of the new exemption schedule. Consequently, if you, the run-of-the-mill taxpayer, have plans of dying, do so before midnight, December 31, 2010, or your estate may well return to the old exemption status like a hangover come New Year's Day morning, 2011.

## THROWING AWAY PRECIOUS TAX EXEMPTIONS

For years nearly every married couple has managed to squander one of its two available estate tax exemptions by holding assets in joint or co-ownership, with the names of both husband and wife appearing on the titles and deeds of the assets.

The Internal Revenue Service looks upon joint ownership as separate and unrelated estates. As an example: John and Mary Smith have a total estate of $1.8 million that they hold in joint ownership. Uncle Sam, however, says that John has a $900,000 estate and Mary has a $900,000 estate. And what a whale of a difference this makes. When one of the spouses dies, his available exemption must be used to pass his half of the estate ($900,000) to the surviving spouse, just as if the assets were being passed to the kids or any other heir.

Now, with one spouse dead, the entire $1.8 million estate is in the sole ownership of Mary, the surviving spouse. Joint ownership is terminated and, most important, one of the couple's $1.5 million estate tax exemptions has been used up.

When the surviving spouse also dies, she will have only her $1.5 million exemption left to shelter her now solely owned $1.8 million estate from estate taxes. There will be a $300,000 excess on which the surviving spouse's estate will have to pay $117,000 in federal estate taxes; money that could have easily gone to John and Mary's children had the couple used their two exemptions wisely.

## THE TAX-SAVING A-B LIVING TRUST

A much more intelligent use by John and Mary of their available exemptions would be to employ what is known as an *A-B living trust.*

Up until now we have been discussing what is known as a "common" living trust. When used by a married couple, each spouse is a co-grantor (maker) of a common trust. When one spouse dies, the survivor becomes the sole grantor and trustee of the trust in much the same way that joint ownership turns into sole ownership when one spouse dies. The survivor gains full control and has the right to change or amend any part of a common living trust in any way he chooses. But he also loses one of the couple's two estate tax exemptions!

By adding several special paragraphs to a common living trust contract at the time it is drawn, a husband and wife can give each other permission to split the trust evenly into two sub-trusts when one of

# Creating an A-B Living Trust

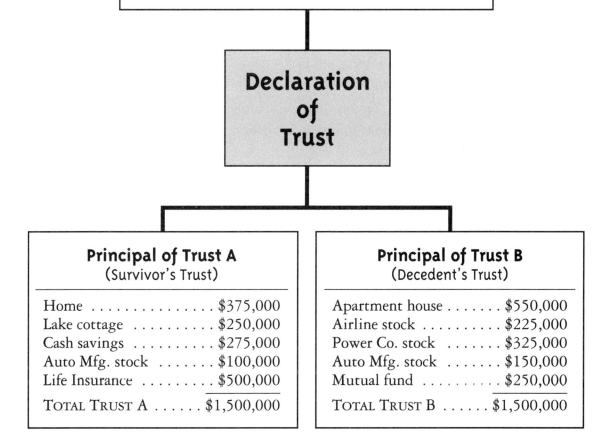

**Principal of the Common Living Trust**

| | |
|---|---|
| Home | $375,000 |
| Apartment house | $550,000 |
| Lake cottage | $250,000 |
| Power Co. stock | $325,000 |
| Auto Mfg. stock | $250,000 |
| Airline stock | $225,000 |
| Mutual fund | $250,000 |
| Cash savings | $275,000 |
| Life insurance | $500,000 |
| TOTAL ESTATE | $3,000,000 |

**Declaration of Trust**

**Principal of Trust A**
(Survivor's Trust)

| | |
|---|---|
| Home | $375,000 |
| Lake cottage | $250,000 |
| Cash savings | $275,000 |
| Auto Mfg. stock | $100,000 |
| Life Insurance | $500,000 |
| TOTAL TRUST A | $1,500,000 |

**Principal of Trust B**
(Decedent's Trust)

| | |
|---|---|
| Apartment house | $550,000 |
| Airline stock | $225,000 |
| Power Co. stock | $325,000 |
| Auto Mfg. stock | $150,000 |
| Mutual fund | $250,000 |
| TOTAL TRUST B | $1,500,000 |

them dies—one for each spouse (in John and Mary's case, approximately $900,000 is placed in each sub-trust).

The survivor's trust is known as Trust A, while the decedent's trust is known as Trust B. (An easy way to remember which is which is by associating Trust A with "Alive" spouse and Trust B with "Buried" spouse. This is perhaps a bit crass, but from the standpoint of practicality it gets the job done.)

The A-B trust establishes that the survivor is in fact only the manager of Trust B and not entitled to unrestricted dips in its principal. The exemption of the first spouse to die can be used to shelter Trust B from estate taxes, while the survivor's exemption is put on hold and reserved to shelter Trust A when the survivor eventually passes. The couple can now take full advantage of both of their exemptions and pass up to twice as much to their heirs completely free of federal estate taxes.

With an A-B living trust, when John dies, his $900,000 is placed in Trust B, completely sheltered from any estate taxes under the current exemption schedule. But in this scenario, when Mary eventually dies, the $900,000 in her Trust A is also sheltered from estate taxes. Their children receive the full amount, estate tax–free.

The increase in the exemption between now and 2010 will accomplish the following for married couples holding their assets in an A-B living trust:

| ESTATE TAX EXEMPTIONS WITH AN A-B LIVING TRUST |
| --- |
| **January 1, 2004** . . . . . . . . . $3,000,000 total exemption per married couple |
| **January 1, 2006** . . . . . . . . . $4,000,000 total exemption per married couple |
| **January 1, 2009** . . . . . . . . . $7,000,000 total exemption per married couple |

This ability of an A-B living trust to double the amount of your available estate tax exemption (especially at these new rates) should be reason enough to abandon joint ownership of assets immediately and get into a living trust.

# Using Estate Tax Exemptions of Both Spouses

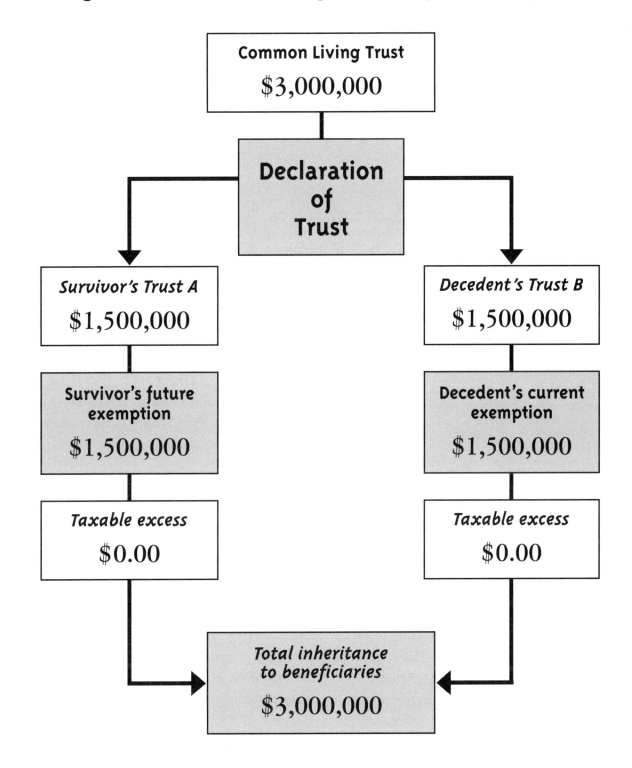

# Additional Benefits

There are other major advantages to an A-B trust:

1. The surviving spouse can spend both principal and income from her own Trust A in any manner, without restrictions.

2. The surviving spouse is permitted to spend all income earned by Trust B such as interest and dividends, plus the greater of five thousand dollars or five percent of principal in Trust B every year in any manner, no matter how foolishly.

3. In addition to the yearly five thousand dollars or five percent of principal that can be spent in any manner from Trust B, the surviving spouse is also permitted to spend unlimited sums of principal from Trust B for education, health care, and to maintain the lifestyle enjoyed during the marriage. In most marriages, that would mean that the surviving spouse could also use the principal from Trust B for such lifestyle-maintaining expenses as buying a new car, paying the rent, remodeling the kitchen, putting a new roof on the house, taking a conventional vacation, and other similar expenditures. The surviving spouse, as trustee of Trust B has access to any of the Trust B assets according to IRS rules. However, the IRS would frown upon using funds from Trust B to speculate or to purchase some luxury item such as a condo in Cancun. The expenditures are generally monitored by the beneficiaries themselves (those for whom the Trust B assets are eventually destined) to make sure that such assets are being used only for legitimate purposes.

4. Trust B becomes irrevocable upon the death of the first spouse and cannot be changed at the whim of the survivor (perhaps through the influence of a new spouse), as can happen with either a will or a common trust. Thus, the rights of the deceased spouse are protected even in death.

5. The A-B trust is also ideal for couples on their second marriages. Each spouse, using a special memorandum, can place assets in the trust for the mutual enjoyment and use of both, but upon death must come out of the trust and be returned to the heirs of the first marriage.

*Put not your trust in money, but put your money in trust.*

—OLIVER WENDELL HOLMES

As an example of that last point: Jean and Jerry, both widowed, decide to marry. Jerry's first marriage produced no children. However, Jean has a child from her first marriage. Both Jerry and Jean decide to place the assets gained in their first marriages in an A-B living trust. Jerry simply transfers his assets into the trust; however, Jean places hers in the trust through a memorandum that states that upon her death, those assets must be returned to the child of her first marriage. In contrast, both Jerry's assets from his first marriage and those accumulated during the second marriage will be divided into Trusts A and B upon his death.

## The Mechanics of an A-B Living Trust

Granted, introducing the notion of splitting a living trust into two sub-trusts seems to add a degree of complexity to the living trust concept. However, be assured that the creation and maintenance of an A-B living trust is simple and easy.

A common living trust becomes an A-B living trust by adding several special paragraphs to the trust contract at the time it is written. In this specially added text, each spouse gives the other permission to split the assets into two sub-trusts immediately after the death of the first spouse. These additional paragraphs also set down the conditions as to how the two sub-trusts must operate. This language then lays dormant in the trust contract until the death of one spouse.

The split is made by the surviving spouse *after* the other's death. The division is of a bookkeeping nature only; the shared trust assets do not need to be re-titled into the two separate trusts. Rather, the assets are divided into two separate lists, one labeled Trust A (the survivor's trust) and the other Trust B (the decedent's trust). The survivor divides the assets as equally as possible. Each list must also contain a reasonable estimated value of each asset and a basis from which the estimate was made. Bank accounts, CDs, and similar assets are easy to evaluate. You need only check with the bank or consult your passbook or online banking. Other assets, such as stocks and real estate, require a little more effort. The value of a stock can be determined simply by attaching the

## SAMPLE CONTENT FROM AN A-B LIVING TRUST DOCUMENT

The death of one of the grantors shall cause the trust to be divided into two parts by the surviving trustee.

One such part to be known as the decedent's share and referred to hereinafter as Trust B shall consist first of all assets held as separate property within the common Trust by the deceased grantor. After consideration of all funeral, burial, final illness, and legal expenses and of all amounts outside of this Trust passing to heirs through probate procedure, such community property shall be divided as equally as possible, one part, not to exceed the available unified credit to avoid Federal Estate Taxes upon the deceased grantor's total estate being added to Trust B. Upon this division of the assets, Trust B shall be considered irrevocable.

The second part to be known as the survivor's share and referred to hereinafter as Trust A shall consist of assets held as separate property in the common Trust by the surviving grantor together with the remainder of jointly-held assets from the common Trust including any life insurance proceeds on the life of the deceased grantor.

The trustee shall manage both Trusts A and B according to the Conditions and Terms of Trust administration of the common Trust.

During the lifetime of the surviving grantor, the trustee shall pay to the surviving grantor the income of the Trust Estate from Trust A and such portions of the principal of Trust A as the surviving grantor from time to time directs, or as otherwise directed by the surviving grantor, or as it may appear necessary for the welfare, comfort and maintenance of customary lifestyle of the surviving grantor during physical or mental incompetence.

During the lifetime of the surviving grantor, the trustee shall pay to the surviving grantor the income from Trust B in quarterly or, when convenient, more frequent payments.

At the sole discretion of the trustee, the principal of Trust B shall be distributed to beneficiaries according to the terms of the Schedule of Trust Beneficiaries or distributed as the trustee deems necessary to the surviving grantor for the health, education, and maintenance of lifestyle to which the surviving grantor has become accustomed.

At the sole discretion of the trustee, a sum of $5,000 from Trust B or 5 percent of the market value of the Trust Estate held in Trust B as valued by the latest regular annual valuation of the Trust's assets may also be made available annually to the surviving grantor to use in any way the surviving grantor so chooses. Such an entitlement shall not be cumulative from any year to another.

The trustee shall have the right to resign the Trusteeship of either or both A and B Trusts at any time. Upon the resignation of the trustee, the successor trustee shall appropriately assume active management of either or both A and B Trusts as may be required by such resignation.

Upon the certification and request of the personal representative or administrator of the deceased grantor's estate, the trustee shall reimburse from Trust B the said personal representative or administrator for all funeral, burial, last illness, and probate expense lawfully allowed in the settlement of the deceased grantor's estate. In the absence of probate proceedings, the trustee shall settle such claims from the Trust Estate.

The trustee shall pay or reimburse from Trust B the personal representative or administrator of the deceased grantor's estate for the amount of certified estate or inheritance taxes lawfully levied by federal, state, or local governments as a result of the death of the deceased grantor.

Upon the death of the surviving grantor the trustee shall:

(A) Reimburse the personal representative or administrator of the surviving grantor's estate for all legal funeral expenses and the expenses of any final illness as certified and requested by such personal representative or administrator. In the absence of any probate proceedings, the trustee shall see to the settlement of any such claims along with any other outstanding indebtedness, private or commercial, of the Trust.

(B) Add any balance of principal and income remaining in Trust B to the balance of principal and income in Trust A and distribute the combined Trust Estate according to the instructions in the Schedule of Trust Beneficiaries.

*The avoidance of taxes is the only intellectual pursuit that carries any reward.*

—JOHN MAYNARD KEYNES

daily newspaper stock market report to the list and circling the value of the stock on that particular day. To estimate the value of a piece of real estate, attach the written appraisals of three local realtors to the list and take an average.

This split of the assets is not written in granite. The surviving trustee is allowed at any time in the future to swap assets back and forth between the two sub-trusts so long as the trade is always made current-dollar-value for current-dollar-value. To make an exchange, you must again attach to each list an authorized basis for the assets you are trading, such as stock market reports or real estate appraisals, to insure they are of equal value. Note also that unless specifically forbidden in the trust contract, the trustee (surviving spouse) can sell any asset from Trust B but is required to return the funds from the sale to Trust B (plus, profits from the sale may be subject to capital gains taxes).

### The Double Taxation Factor

Why would you want to make a trade of assets from Trust A to Trust B? Again this is one of the advantages of a living trust. The total net worth of Trust B is exposed to government taxation at the time of death of the first spouse. From that moment in time, the federal government can never again hit the trust with estate taxes, even if Trust B grows to astronomical proportions. Any such additional assessment of taxes would be unlawful double taxation.

Let's suppose that your Trust A contains a scrub lot out in the boondocks that for years has been raising nothing but weeds and grasshoppers. In fact, you would be happy to sell it for a song but no one is singing. Suddenly, a huge shopping mall is to be built right across the street from your scrub lot. The new development will inflate the value of your property to an over-the-moon amount and, if left in Trust A, will sadly affect your estate taxes upon your death. However, it won't mean a thing if you swap your lot into Trust B for something of current equal value from Trust B. In Trust B, your scrub lot could safely appreciate by thousands of additional dollars without affecting your estate taxes by one dime.

When making the original split of the trust assets into Trusts A and B, the surviving spouse should be aware of this double taxation factor. As a general tax rule, speculative assets should go in Trust B while the blue-chip, slow growth assets should be placed in Trust A. Also remember that the death of either spouse may be years away. Times, taxes, and politicians change as the years go by. Hence, it is always wise to seek the advice of a tax accountant when it comes time to split assets into A and B sub-trusts.

## Beware of Substitutes

Attorneys have a whole suitcase full of A-B living trust substitutes, each of which is much more complex and does not offer all of the advantages of an A-B living trust. They are generally designed to financially benefit the attorney rather than the client. Perhaps the most infamous of these is the supposedly necessary separate trust for each spouse.

Separate trusts, from the client's standpoint, are a nightmare to administer. Loans are harder to obtain, for each spouse appears to have fewer assets than when combined. Furthermore, after the death of a spouse, the surviving spouse has far less access to the assets in the decedent's trust than she would have to assets in a Trust B derived from an A-B living trust.

Why do many attorneys push the idea of two separate trusts for a married couple rather than one A-B living trust? Just as the supermarket charges more for two quarts of milk than one quart of milk, the attorney can charge more for two trusts than for one trust. Thus, if you insist on having an attorney do your estate planning, stand your ground and demand a government-approved A-B living trust.

Without question, the A-B living trust is more complex than a common living trust. There are no additional complexities while the two spouses are alive. However, upon the death of one spouse, the A-B living trust calls for a greater degree of time and administration from the survivor. Also, due to increased exemptions, estate taxes no longer bear the threat to the average estate they once did. Therefore, if you are 1) absolutely sure that upon one spouse's death the net amount of your

*People who complain about taxes can be divided into two classes: men and women.*

—Unknown

estate, including the face value of life insurance policies, will not exceed the current individual exemption and 2) you are comfortable with giving your spouse complete control of the total net assets in the estate after your death, then there really is no need to consider an A-B living trust. You may want to give the survivor a break and stay with a common living trust.

# GIFT TAXES

Gift taxes are closely related to estate taxes. They are an outside line-backer inserted into the lineup by the government to tackle citizens attempting to make an end run around estate taxes. In other words, if you try to give all or most of your assets away before you die to prevent paying estate taxes, the government will nail you for gift taxes. And because all transactions over ten thousand dollars must be reported to the government by the financial custodian, they've got you, coming or going.

## Staying Within Your Life Exemption

In effect, each person has a life exemption equal to the amount of one's federal estate tax exemption the year one dies. This upper limit is considered to be the maximum amount of gifts that one can give and inheritances that one can bequeath, both before and after death, without paying any gift or estate taxes.

Currently, however, each person or spouse can make gifts of up to eleven thousand dollars every year to as many people as they wish without said gift being deducted from the total amount of that life exemption. It is called the annual exclusion. However, any excess over the eleven thousand dollars given to any one person in any one year will reduce your estate tax exemption at death a like amount.

For example: in the year 2004, you gave your niece the gift of $150,000. Subtracting the $11,000 maximum gift without penalty of tax leaves $139,000. Should you die in 2004, your $1,500,000 estate tax exemption will be reduced by $139,000 down to $1,361,000.

There are a few other exceptions to gifts that are deducted from your lifetime maximum gift exemption in addition to the annual exclusion.

- tuition or medical expenses you pay for someone

- gifts to your spouse

- gifts made to political organizations

- gifts to qualified charities

- charitable remainder trusts

If you want to make a substantial gift to a charity, it may make sense to explore a special kind of trust called a *charitable remainder trust*. It lets you donate generously to charity, and it gives you and your heirs a big tax break.

The most common type of charitable trust is called a charitable remainder trust. First, you set up an irrevocable trust and transfer to it the property that you want to donate to a charity. The charity must be approved by the IRS, which usually means it has tax-exempt status under the Internal Revenue Code. (You can ask the IRS whether or not a particular charity is eligible.)

The charity serves as trustee of the trust, and manages or invests the property so that it will produce income for you. The charity pays you (or anyone else you name) a portion of the income generated by the trust property for a certain number of years or for your whole life. You specify the payment period in the trust document. Then, upon your death or at the end of the period you set, the property goes to the charity.

In addition to helping out your favorite charity, you get several big tax advantages from this arrangement:

- You can take an income tax deduction, over five years, for the value of your gift to the charity. The gift need not be cash. It can be a home, a business, a block of stock, or almost anything of value. Where things get tricky is in determining the amount of your deduction. The value of your gift is not simply the value of the property. The IRS deducts from that value the amount of income that you're likely to receive from the property. For example, if you donate $100,000 but, based on your life expectancy, interest rates, and how the trust document is set up, you might expect to get $25,000 in income back, the value of your gift is really $75,000.

- When your trust property eventually goes to the charity outright (upon your death or the end of the payment period you specify), it's no longer part of your estate—so it isn't subject to federal estate tax.

- You can turn appreciated property (property that has gone up significantly in value since you acquired it) into cash without paying tax on the profit. If you simply sold the property, you would have to pay capital gains tax on your profit. But charities, unlike individuals, don't have to pay capital gains tax. So if you give the property to the trust and the charity sells it, the proceeds stay in the trust and aren't taxed.

## GENERATION-SKIPPING TAXES

Just as with the gift tax, the generation-skipping tax (GST) was designed by Congress to plug any loopholes in the estate tax system. It decrees that any trust set up in any way to distribute benefits to grandchildren or a lower generation will be subject to the maximum penalty set by law.

Just like the estate tax and the gift tax, generation-skipping taxes are to be fully phased out in the year 2010. However, if the tax code that temporarily passed muster in 2001 is not permanently approved by the year 2011, the level falls back to its 2001 plateau of fifty-five percent.

There are few if any escape hatches in the generation-skipping tax law. Anything that even comes close to smacking of a distribution to a generation lower than your own children will be caught in the crunch.

| GENERATION-SKIPPING TAXES THROUGH 2011 | | |
|---|---|---|
| **Year** | **Tax Rate** | **Exemption per spouse** |
| 2004 | 48 percent | $1,500,000 |
| 2005 | 47 percent | $1,500,000 |
| 2006 | 46 percent | $2,000,000 |
| 2007 | 45 percent | $2,000,000 |
| 2008 | 45 percent | $2,000,000 |
| 2009 | 45 percent | $3,500,000 |
| 2010 | 0 percent | Generation-skipping law phased out |
| 2011 | 55 percent | $1,000,000 |

Thankfully, however, there are hefty generation-skipping tax exemptions that await the living trust grantor. If total contributions to grandchildren or lower generations at death are less than the schedule above, there will be no generation-skipping tax. Also, if the parent (your child) of the grandchild has died there will be no generation-skipping tax.

Approximately ninety-seven percent of Americans pay no estate taxes, gift taxes, or generation-skipping taxes. Their estates are small enough to be covered by the available exemptions. That percentage will undoubtedly rise between now and 2010. Knowing the rules and having a living trust can protect estates worth several million dollars from the clutches of Uncle Sam. It is suggested that you review this chapter as many times as necessary to keep you in the majority.

# 7

# Added Blessings, Boons— and Tribulations

I realize that the dimensions of most readers' estates are of modest size and that their intent is to distribute their estates to their children as expediently and inexpensively as prudent judgement allows. However, the living trust offers many additional possibilities that are worth exploring.

## CHILDREN'S TRUST

When at long last the probate carnival has concluded, the court has few alternatives. By law, probate court must distribute without delay what is left of the assets to the legal heirs. Probate court has no structure or authority to hold a portion of such assets for later distribution—nor to determine which heirs might not as yet be competent or mature enough to manage their windfall intelligently. Bequests left via a will to minor children and managed for a number of years by a court conservator must be turned over immediately in a lump sum to the child at legal age, no strings attached. Who among us has not known a psychologically immature youth of legal age who suddenly inherited a large sum of money, only to squander it in a matter of months on tawdry pleasures?

With a living trust, however, the grantor has almost boundless alternatives. Parents (trust grantors) are able to set up children's sub-trusts within the original document, instructing the successor trustee to distribute the principal of the trust to the children over several payments: perhaps a third at age twenty-one, another third at age twenty-five, and a final distribution of the remainder at age thirty. In this way, much of the estate continues within the trust to enjoy the advantages of both expert management and inflation, eventually being worth several times its value had it been distributed immediately upon the death of the surviving parent. Hence, parents might choose not to distribute the principal but instead perpetuate the living trust by investing the funds in an income mutual fund that will pay each of their children a monthly "pension" for the rest of their lives.

## PHYSICAL INCAPACITY AND MENTAL INCOMPETENCE

*"I've got all the money I'll ever need if I die by four o'clock this afternoon."*

—HENNY YOUNGMAN

The provisions listed in a will cannot kick into gear until the maker of the will dies. The maker of a will can be disabled, destitute, and delirious, but until he is dead the will serves only to collect dust in a dark drawer or safe. Such human problems as incompetence, caring for minor children, provisions for catastrophic illness, and other "still alive but feebly kicking" dilemmas are unresolvable with a will.

In contrast, the living trust is truly a dynamic agent that can often be as valuable during the lifetime of the grantor as it is upon his death. Upon the notarizing of the signature on the trust declaration, the document roles up its sleeves and goes to work on the spot. The fear of humiliating probate incompetence hearings held in your behalf, along with their usual disastrous verdicts, is negated.

Your living trust can provide a much more palatable passageway and functional mode for dealing with this valid potentiality. Your living trust can list two or three doctors—people of integrity whom you have known and trusted for years—personally selected by you during healthier times to determine your competence and capacity should it ever be challenged.

| PHYSICAL AND MENTAL INCAPACITY | | |
| --- | --- | --- |
| | **Wills** | **Trusts** |
| **Determination of incapacity** | Public hearing at courthouse; judge determines if person is incompetent and appoints conservator to manage assets | Two doctors, privately appointed by trust grantor, determine mental or physical incapacity |
| **Management of assets during incapacity** | Assets under the public management of probate court through the court-appointed conservator | Assets privately managed by successor trustee(s) of the living trust |
| **Guardianship of minor children** | Guardian appointed in will must be approved by probate court | Guardian appointed in pour-over will must be approved by probate court |
| **Management of minor children's assets** | Court-appointed conservator manages assets | Assets privately managed by successor trustee(s) of the living trust |
| **Legal recovery** | Public hearing again in probate court. Grantor is on his own to secure witnesses that will establish his right to be restored to legal competency | Same two-doctor team reexamines the grantor and, finding a recovery, restores the grantor to full control over trust assets |

Should the doctors determine that you are unable to continue proficient control of your affairs, your personally designated and faithful successor trustee will step in and capably handle your responsibilities until such time as you are once again able to resume your duties. There are no courtroom histrionics, no alien attorneys, no prying judges or juries, no outsiders meddling in your private business, and no embarrassing notices in the local newspaper advising every wagging tongue in town that you are currently a few bricks short of a full load.

Nor does the reversal of the procedure bring on a probate calamity pitting you against what would not only seem to be the whole world, but your own family, too. You simply ask that same team of trusted professional people to reexamine you. If their conclusion supports a recovery, *by law* your successor trustee must step aside into the wings and allow you once again to occupy full stage, totally in command of your affairs.

---

### Guardianship of Minors in the Case of Incapacity

Upon the physical or mental incapacity of the grantor(s), the appointment of a grantor-selected personal guardian for minor children is easily handled within the confines of a *pour-over will,* an auxiliary document accompanying a living trust, discussed later in this chapter. It is entirely possible to name guardians for your children in your living trust contract itself (or any other document, for that matter). However, as has already been pointed out, your selection of a guardian must receive the blessing of probate court. Appointing guardians in your living trust contract will open that document to the prying eyes of probate court. Therefore, the document of choice in which to name guardians is your pour-over will, which already has the scrutiny of the court.

---

## "Q-TIP" OR A-B-C TRUSTS

It is not within the scope of this book to explain the full advantages of adding a Trust C to the dimension of an A-B living trust. The use of a Trust C (called a Qualified Terminal Property Trust and often referred to as a "Q-Tip Trust") is generally restricted to married couples with total net assets in excess of the current exemption for a married couple upon the time of death of both spouses.

To prevent the payment of any estate taxes upon the death of the first spouse, the full amount of net assets allowed a married couple under the current exemption is split and placed equally in Trust A and Trust B. The surplus in the estate over the total exemption is then placed in a Trust C. With both Trusts A and B under the exemption amount, the total payment of any estate taxes on Trust C is deferred until after the death of the second spouse. Deft but legal income juggling in the years between the two deaths can often transcribe into substantial tax savings.

An example: Melvin and Margaret have a total estate of $4 million in 2004, placing them $1 million over their total marriage exemption of $3 million. Upon Melvin's death, Margaret places their $4 million in an A-B-C trust as follows:

Trust A: $1,500,000
Trust B: $1,500,000
Trust C: $1,000,000

Margaret will see to it that all future profits go into Trust C. The plan does not cut estate taxes by one penny. It does have the advantage of delaying the payment of estate taxes until the surviving spouse is dead. When Margaret passes on, all assets in Trust C will be subject to the estate tax at the year of her death.

The intricate strategy involved in the employment of Trust C is outside the realm of any living trust guidance manual or kit. Readers who find themselves in this prestigious but minute minority certainly have the resources to avail themselves, along with their obviously more complicated affairs, of the in-person services of qualified nearby estate planners and tax consultants. I urge you to hustle off to such professionals at your earliest opportunity.

## AUXILIARY DOCUMENTS

There is no one magical document that can cure all ills within its pages, and the living trust contract is no exception. Thus, all living trusts should be supported by several auxiliary documents that cover a few minor gaps in a person's estate plan. A pour-over will is almost a necessity and limited powers of attorney for both financial needs and health care follow close behind. Let me now spell out the urgency to include each of these in your living trust package.

# The Pour-Over Will

No matter how hard you try or how painstaking you are in making sure all of your assets are safely re-titled in the name of your living trust, there is always the chance that something will be left out. Perhaps the vacant lot next to the house you inherited when your parents died or perhaps the balance on a note due to you by some forgotten debtor may escape your detection. And there are always those final paychecks, last-minute dividends, rent payments from tenants, and Social Security checks that may not make it into your trust banking account before your demise. You might even inherit a valuable piece of real estate when you are close enough to the end of the trail to prevent you from placing it in your trust.

Consider also the possibility of you and your spouse dying at the same time as the result of an accident due to someone else's negligence. Any cash award made by an insurance company would be paid to your estate and, without some very adroit juggling, would probably require probate.

## Simplifying the Process

As a protective backup, a well-drawn living trust will always include a pour-over will. This is an instrument to catch those inadvertent oversights that would otherwise have to undergo the sorry spectacle, nuisance and expense of an intestate probate procedure. Without a pour-over will, the state in which you live would distribute these forgotten assets based on that state's laws (refer back to Chapter 2).

The pour-over will is far less complicated than the normal will used to transfer an entire estate through the probate technique. A personal representative (executor) must be named in the pour-over will; however, to streamline their affairs, many trust grantors name their successor trustee as their personal representative should a probate action be necessary. The pour-over will names your living trust as the sole heir, and thus, when probate of those forgotten assets is concluded, they will flow, though belatedly, into your living trust and become subject to the same schedule of distribution commanded by your living trust.

> ### A Word of Advice
> It is worth noting that there have been a few cases where a facile successor trustee armed with a skillfully drawn living trust has convinced a probate judge that it was the clear intent of the decedent to place all assets into the trust. When granted the authority to do so by probate court, backup trustees have actually placed assets into living trusts after the grantors had passed on. However, such instances are rare and should not be relied on. I make the point here only to emphasize the significance of having a clear and comprehensive living trust document that lucidly spells out your intentions and goals.

## Appointing Guardians for Underage Children

As previously mentioned, the pour-over will is the proper vehicle in which to name guardians for children. Guardians and conservators must always be approved by probate court. The appointment can be made in almost any document, even the trust contract. However, naming such appointees in your living trust document could open your entire trust to the prying eyes of that court. Therefore, it makes much more sense to place such nominees in a document that is already in the clutches of probate, which in this case is the pour-over will.

Again, because the gears of a will cannot intermesh until its maker has passed on, minor children of a surviving, but incapacitated parent will soon be placed under the supervision of probate court. The court-appointed guardian in charge of the children might not necessarily meet with the approval of an incompetent parent; however, she is in no condition to formulate any degree of judgment.

## Disinheriting Children

The pour-over will is also a useful device for disinheriting disfavored children. Both living trusts and standard Last Will and Testaments always list beneficiaries or heirs along with the assets they are to inherit, and are rarely cluttered with the names of those that are being left nothing. Listing the disfavored is like rubbing their noses in the fact that they are receiving little or nothing and can create a great deal of family animosity and ill will.

Astonishingly, there are many instances on record where disinherited children have made successful challenges to wills by claiming that they were inadvertently forgotten. For this reason, the pour-over will often awards all of the grantors' children, along with all grandchildren, the sum of one dollar each of any assets inadvertently left outside the trust. This accomplishes the task of recording the names of each of your descendants and eliminating the possibility that a disinherited child (or the children of a deceased disinherited child) could claim that she was unintentionally forgotten. When a disfavored child is remembered for the sum of one dollar in the pour-over will, but mysteriously comes up missing from the list of beneficiaries named within the living trust document, there can be no doubt as to the grantor's true intentions.

## The Durable Financial Power of Attorney

A well-designed living trust will also include a durable financial power of attorney. Like the pour-over will, this is a separate document that exists outside of the living trust.

A durable financial power of attorney, when combined with a living trust, is basically a document of convenience. This power is usually given to your successor trustee, although you may name anyone you choose or as many as you choose for this role.

Your Declaration of Trust gives your spouse, as the co-grantor, the power to act for you in the affairs of the trust. Financially, nothing else is needed. However, when there is no co-grantor to take action, the giving of durable power of attorney to your successor trustee can allow him, now as your attorney-in-fact (sometimes referred to as an agent), to transfer any belated or forgotten assets into your living trust should you be incapacitated, out of the country, or otherwise unavailable. Understand that without such agency your successor trustee has no authority over the assets that you hold outside the trust.

As an example: Fresh and happy on Monday morning, you set out to transfer your assets into your new living trust. Tuesday at noon, with the job half-completed, you are felled by a stroke and cannot finish the job, putting the clamps on the creation of your living trust. In such a case, the giving of a financial power of attorney to your successor trustee can permit him to step in and conclude the task of transferring assets to the trust. Without such an auxiliary document, your successor trustee is helpless and your trust is stuck in the mud.

As grantors of a living trust, the accompanying durable powers of attorney given your agent are generally limited to the transfer of property into your living trust. The actual management of the trust (purchasing, selling, paying taxes and such) can be easily handled by your successor trustee under the conditions of the living trust contract should you become incapacitated. Thus, there is no need to grant the unlimited powers of attorney that can sometimes lead to the raiding of an estate by less-than-honorable relatives or friends.

In most instances, grantors name their successor trustee as their attorney-in-fact, which not only cuts confusion, but tends to coordinate all responsibilities under the hat of the same person.

## Health Care Power of Attorney

Many attorneys and estate planners also include a living will or health care power of attorney in the trust package. However, both are auxiliary documents and not a part of the trust. These documents legally allow health care decisions to be made for you should you become physically or mentally incapable of making such decisions for yourself.

Although the terms living will and health care power of attorney are used interchangeably, officially there is a great deal of difference. A living will gives a health care provider, such as a hospital or doctor, the legal authority to make health care decisions for you—including the right to make life-sustaining decisions (generally referred to as "pulling the plug"). Both doctors and hospitals shy away from this responsibility. So much in fact that living wills are now illegal in most states. In its place has come the health care power of attorney, in which the maker of the document (the patient) appoints a patient advocate, such as a relative, friend or associate, to make such decisions when the patient, because of physical or mental incapacity, is unable to make such decisions for himself.

There is a great deal of misunderstanding in America concerning health care power of attorney documents. Many people believe such a document allows the patient advocate to demand certain medical procedures, medicines, and the "pulling of the plug." Not so! All the patient advocate can do is make a request. The doctor and the hospital also have rights; on the basis of their own moral and religious convictions they can refuse to carry out the patient advocate's wishes. Millions of dollars in lawsuits are wasted each year by families attempting to force a doctor or hospital to comply with the patient advocate's demands. They do not reckon with the realization that doctors and hospitals will always win such legal battles simply on the grounds of violating their civil rights—they cannot be forced to naturally or unnaturally terminate a life.

Therefore, filling out a health care power of attorney and appointing a patient advocate is only one-half the battle. You must now engage your doctor in a heart-to-heart to make sure that his religious and ethical values and those of the hospital where he practices are in complete accordance with yours. If not, to give teeth to your health care power of attorney, you are now faced with the job of changing doctors.

Living wills and health care power of attorney documents are usually available at local physician's offices and hospitals free of charge. Because the laws of all fifty states vary dramatically when it comes to the regulation of such health care decisions, it seems the much wiser choice to avail oneself of this gratis service and know that you are getting the very latest document designed especially for your particular state.

# WHAT YOUR LIVING TRUST *CAN'T* DO: DODGING THE COST OF LONG-TERM CARE

Long-term nursing home care and the living trust have produced more than their share of myths and rumors.

There is a great deal of wishful thinking among seniors in America that a living trust can somehow reduce or even totally eliminate the cost of nursing home care that can hit a family like a Boeing 747 falling in the backyard.

Many seniors reason that if the assets are owned by the trust, they are then indeed paupers, which automatically qualifies them to have Medicaid pay for their care at a nursing home. This logic overlooks one important factor: living trusts are almost always *revocable* trusts. That means that the grantor of the trust has immediate access to the trust and its assets and may make any changes she wishes. Further translation then tells us that the grantor of the trust has the full ability to invade the trust assets and do with them as she pleases: spend them, distribute them, sell them, or buy more of them. Therefore the government says that for nursing home purposes the assets are still indeed controlled by the grantor and can be included in the total assets of her estate.

The various state and federal governments have all reached the conclusion that funds saved for a rainy day should be used for a rainy day and not for purchasing a forty-foot motor home, luxury houseboat, or hacienda in Puerto Vallarta. Slowly and surely the government has been shutting off the remaining loopholes that in the past have allowed the well-to-do to plead poverty when the time came to move to a nursing home. Right or wrong, the government controls the purse strings to the government treasury and those who don't agree to play by the rules don't receive Medicaid from the government.

However, this has not stopped misleading newspaper ads, direct mail flyers, and hotel and restaurant seminars given by hucksters who imply that they have a secret plan or trick trust that will do the job. Investigation invariably turns up that these miracle long-term care cost cures are either 1) an irrevocable trust in which the trust maker loses all control over his assets, 2) deeding all the assets to the children, or 3) an insurance policy that the charlatan just happens to have for sale.

Yet, after hearing these truths time and again, too many seniors still tragically continue to chase the carrot the moment some stranger on the next lunch-counter stool whispers that a friend of a friend's great Aunt Susie, worth a half-million, got into a plan that enticed Medicaid to pay one hundred percent of her nursing home care while she spent the half-million betting on the ponies.

## Medicaid: A Complex and Confusing System

Great misunderstanding engulfs the Medicaid system. Many people believe that once the government finds the assets they have hidden, the Medicaid constabulary snatches them away and applies them to their nursing home costs. Not true. The government does not snatch anything.

Instead, every person applying for Medicaid assistance in paying for long-term care undergoes a complete financial investigation. If assets are found that exceed near-pauperism, or if it's discovered that in recent years the applicant finagled a few deals to lower his worth and defraud the government into paying for his long-term care, the applicant still gets to keep everything he owns. Nothing changes. No one snatches money out of his bank account. He just doesn't get any money from the state to pay for his board at a nursing home.

The state simply tells the applicant: "Medicaid is for the impoverished. You want to go to a nursing home? You've got the money to pay for it yourself. When your money is nearly gone, come back and see us and we will take another look."

The fact that the applicant was going to use his savings to buy a second home in sunny Arizona or pay his grandchildren's way through college does not sway the government one bit.

Most troublesome is the fact that the Medicaid laws, rulings, and interpretations change each time you cross a state line. You can ask three different experts to recite the rules to you and get three different answers. It is that complex! Medicaid officials themselves from one county to the next within the same state often disagree. And it seems that just about the time you think you have the rules straight, the government changes the rules again.

## Qualifications for Medicaid

To qualify for Medicaid and a monthly pittance to buy shaving cream, shampoo, and a newspaper, the present federal system allows a single person liquid assets totaling not more than approximately $2,000 (excluding a home and a car worth less than $4,500). In the case of a married couple with one spouse living at home and the other requiring long-term care, the liquid asset allowance shoots up to approximately $90,000.

There is a "look back" period of three years (five years for those that have irrevocable trusts) to determine if the applicant has made any unusually large gifts or sold assets at well below fair market value to artificially lower her net worth.

---

### New Federal Laws Regarding Medicaid

Federal laws have been recently passed that allow an unlimited look back if the government suspects that assets have been disposed of for the purpose of qualifying for Medicaid. Thus far, those laws have not been enforced (perhaps because the government may believe them to be unconstitutional). However, it is easy to see where this is leading and it is apparent to most that this will be the next great tightening of the screws.

---

## A Home Remedy Sure to Backfire

Many people try to sidestep the system by deeding away their assets to their children. But even if you succeed in bamboozling the government, you may have built yourself a monster. You may believe that the child to whom you must now look for support is entirely trustworthy. But what if that child dies unexpectedly while you and your spouse are still healthy and living independently? Can your child's widow, widower, or your grandchildren be trusted to abide by the under-the-table agreement you made with your child? You would not have a leg to stand on in court if your grandchildren, daughter-in-law, or son-in-law decided to blow what was once your money on themselves rather than contribute to your support.

Let's say that seniors John and Mary, relatively healthy for their age group, decide to beat the system by deeding all their assets over to their trusted friend Bob, on the under-the-table condition that he turn the assets back over to John and Mary as they need them. Somehow the government overlooks the chicanery but, a few years later, Bob gets run down by a speeding car. Suddenly, all of the assets John and Mary turned over to Bob pass to Bob's children through his will. Bob's children choose not to honor the secret agreement he had made with John and Mary, who are now faced with perhaps another two decades of life sans income. John and Mary have no legal recourse whatsoever. They cannot file suit that there was some clandestine agreement made with their friend Bob to secretly transfer the assets.

---

### An Expensive Solution

Deeding assets wholly to your own children before death is a much greater disservice to the children than giving them joint ownership. The children will lose all possible stepped-up valuation and will be hit with staggering capital gains taxes that may far exceed what was saved by avoiding probate. This should be done only after long and careful consideration.

---

The best possible solution to the problem is to provide long-term care insurance on yourself and your spouse. Granted such insurance is expensive and based on your general health and years of remaining life expectancy. However, the younger you are when you initiate the protection, the less expensive will be the premium. Realize also that the long-term care insurance field is becoming competitive. There are some fairly reasonable insurance buys out there if you take the time to look around.

# 8

# On Your Mark, Get Set, Go

Regardless of whether you employ an attorney to draw your trust or decide to do it yourself with online help, there are various decisions that must first be made as you begin to organize your revocable living trust. If you are single you may want to wrestle with them alone; however, it might be wiser to seek input from those relatives and beneficiaries who will be affected by your living trust. The task is a bit easier when you are married and have the additional wisdom and counsel of your spouse—the very person whose life will be most impacted by those decisions.

## CHOOSING A TRUSTEE

Who will run the show? Obviously, because the grantor(s) and primary beneficiary(s) of the trust are predetermined, the very first decision in the organization of any living trust is choosing who will be the trustee.

Reviewing again the basic objects for having a living trust, we remember that fundamentally we want to save money on both the probate process and possible estate taxes, yet at the same time remain in tight control of our assets. Thus, the primary determination must be if you as grantor(s) of the trust want to be your own trustee(s) or turn this assignment of trust management over to some other person or professional trust-managing firm. Because it is the grantor of the trust that sets down the goals and rules of a revocable trust, while alive she is always the ultimate authority and chief executive regardless of who is named trustee.

## You and/or Your Spouse as Trustees

Thus, the choice between being your own trustee or "hiring the job out" really comes down to a matter of time, costs, and aptitude. For alert and energetic grantors, self-management is a relatively easy task. Such grantors are usually already involved in running a business, holding down a job, or punching a time clock. Most of the wealth accumulated at that stage of a grantor's life has been produced by the sweat of the brow or the gray matter just behind it. He or she simply continues to manage the everyday affairs as always: a nose to the grindstone, a hand to the checkbook, and an eye to safe investments for anything left over after the mortgage, grocery bills, and taxes are paid for.

Where a married couple chooses to be its own trust manager, they almost always decide to do it as co-trustees. Each co-trustee has equal power to act either independently or in tandem as they so choose. This is in keeping with the modern American family philosophy that husband and wife are equal partners in their marriage—each with equal rights. However, it is perfectly legal for either of the spouses to act as sole trustee. In fact, there may be good reasons for doing so, as in the case of the physical or mental incapacity—or the simple lack of financial experience—of one spouse. Husbands or wives that choose to turn over sole trusteeship to their spouse can do so with the peace of mind that as co-grantors, each spouse retains full veto power over any trust decision their trustee spouse might make. Also, the marital laws of most states prevent a wife from being disinherited by a husband in a will or trust unless the wife specifically and knowingly signs her inheritance away before witnesses.

*I love money, but will money ever love me in return?*

—MASON COOLEY

### Divorce

Regardless of which technique is used to title assets, dissolving a marriage is never a pleasant task. To folks not as yet familiar with the mechanics of a living trust, this lesser-used and seemingly obscure technique of titling assets seems to add to the confusion. In fact many husbands and wives whose marriages border on instability are reluctant to enter into a living trust out of fear that it someday might take three Philadelphia lawyers and an elephant to legally pry them apart. However, it must be remembered that divorce is always ninety-five percent negotiation and bartering. Often times such arbitration sinks to the no-holds-barred, bare-knuckle level; nonetheless, it is still mediation between two free human beings and their attorneys as to child custody, future financial help, and the dividing of the assets. Revocable living trusts are easily terminated. The grantors need only reverse the procedure that in the beginning created the trust. Namely, the assets are transferred from trust ownership back into private ownership simply by making that request of the financial custodians. What once took fifteen minutes to create again takes fifteen minutes to put asunder.

Depending on the final resolutions clawed out by the bargaining of the two combatants, any one of several easy scenarios can transpire. Both husband and wife may choose to terminate the trust completely, each taking his or her negotiated individual share and placing it in sole ownership or perhaps a new living trust. One of the two may decide to amend the present trust and buy out the interest of the other or just turn over half the assets to the other. The point is that aborting a living trust is no more difficult than terminating joint ownership of the assets. Therefore, if you are presently dissatisfied with your husband's barber or the way your wife hogs the bathroom and are afraid these minor tiffs will eventually lead to all-out war, do not let it deter you from creating a living trust. It will abrogate as quickly as you created it.

## Trust Companies

At or near retirement, however, lifestyles tend to change. Income is no longer primarily produced by the nine-to-five physical or mental toil of the grantor. Instead, responsibility is geared more to conserving the savings from a lifetime's labor and overseeing the income from a sometimes diversified array of bank savings, stocks, bonds, mutual funds, rental property, retirement pensions and funds, and Social Security. If the grantor has not picked up a sufficient amount of management know-how along the way in such matters, she may feel more comfortable turning family financial affairs over to a person or firm with more fiscal expertise. This can be especially true if the grantor wants to be carefree to travel or just to putter around the house or garden in a relaxed and contented fashion.

*You can be young without money but you can't be old without it.*

—TENNESSEE WILLIAMS

But unless you have a banker, investment broker, accountant, or learned relative that owes you big time, you must expect to pay for these professional or even semi-professional services. Compensation means paying out money, which of course goes against the grain of one of the original objectives of placing your assets within a living trust: saving money! However, as grantor of your own living trust, you may feel that this is a fair trade-off for the personal freedom and the professional service and guidance that such people and firms can supply.

Trust company fees vary from firm to firm and there often are minimums regarding the size of the trust such firms will handle. However, any such trust company will be most happy to discuss its services and fees with you at your convenience. As a general rule, you can expect to pay twenty to forty dollars per thousand annually on estates valued at a million dollars or less. Keep in mind that this charge is a management fee on invested capital only, whether the trust company makes a cent for you or not. You can expect an additional "growth" fee of up to three or four percent on any success they have in multiplying your wealth. Such an arrangement works both ways; the prospect of earning a larger fee is an inducement to the trust company to do a good job for the grantors.

# CHOOSING A SUCCESSOR TRUSTEE

A slightly different rationale is applied to the selection of a successor or "backup" trustee (the person or firm that takes over family financial affairs upon the incapacity or death of the original trustees). All things considered, the same great care should go into the selection of the backup trustee as in the choice of a trustee. You should consider the dexterity of proposed candidates, carefully weighing the duties and the duration of their service.

The overwhelming majority of living trusts are designed to distribute the remaining assets to the contingent beneficiaries as prudently and expediently as possible upon the demise of the surviving grantor. This final distribution terminates the existence of the trust and everyone involved gets back to the business of conducting her own life. It would thus seem that in addition to trustworthiness, the requirements of a successor trustee would be the ability to expediently follow the final instructions of the decedent. She must be able to perform such tasks as:

- paying of the final bills

- filling out the necessary papers and tax returns

- distributing residue from the assets to the beneficiaries as per the grantor's wishes—the total task occupying at most a week or two of the successor trustee's time

Even if such a simple arrangement is your desire, pay heed to the fact that your backup trustee may also be called upon to step in to manage your affairs should you and/or your spouse become incapacitated or incompetent. In such an eventuality, the successor trustee might have to conduct the affairs of the trust for months or even years, a circumstance that will bring into play the successor trustee's long-term administrative proficiency.

## Considerations with Minor Children

The same prospect awaits if the grantor's children are under the age of eighteen at the time of the surviving grantor's death. As you have learned in chapter 3, children under eighteen cannot inherit on their own and any attempt by your trust to place funds other than allowances and expenses in their hands before they are of legal age will serve only to automatically drag probate court into their lives to manage their inheritance until they are of legal age.

Placing a children's trust within the boundaries of your living trust and asking your successor trustee to continue in the management of such a sub-trust extends the existence of your living trust and the continued services of your backup trustee until your children are of legal age—a period that could elongate into a decade or more. In such a case, it may merit your consideration of a professional trust-managing firm with the know-how to administer your longer-range plans. The proficiency of such management firms may be well worth the fee they will charge. After all, the basic expenditure for professional supervision of a quarter-million dollar trust fund will probably be in the range of $5,000 to $10,000 annually plus a fee on any growth in the size of the estate they beget. It is difficult to hire professional help in any field for $100 or so a week.

Professional trust-managing companies are regulated by both state and federal agencies and are geared to follow the objectives of your particular trust without bias or emotion.

They are equipped and trained to stay on top of investment markets and changing regulations. They don't die, move away, take vacations, or become distracted by their own personal concerns and sentiments. Their professionalism has earned them a high degree of respect among the courts and governmental agencies and they remain on call and of service to your loved ones at the touch of a telephone.

## Friends and Family

In the case of a grantor's death after his children have reached legal adulthood, there may be only a few hours of work required of the successor trustee to wind up the trust's affairs. Such being the case, a trusted relative or family friend could well be relied on to execute those concluding details gratuitously. On the other hand, it might be overburdening a lifelong friendship to ask a personal friend-turned-successor-trustee to administer a living trust for an extended period of time without fair compensation. After all, for twelve to twenty-four months of probate-closing assistance, personal representatives named in a conventional will usually expect to be rewarded with one or two percent of the assets.

### Alternate Successor Trustees

Should it appear that the "trusted relative or friend" route be best for you, you should also select at least one alternate. Today you might be willing to trust your life to dear old George, your neighbor next door. But time has a strange way of transforming people, relationships, and situations. Ten years from now—perhaps even ten weeks from now—George may well have moved away, dropped dead of a heart attack, or lost his grip on reality. If George is unavailable or unwilling at the time of your death to serve and you have made no amendments nor named a standby, the matter must be placed before the probate judge who might well appoint *his* next-door neighbor.

## Adult Children as Successor Trustees

Don't overlook your adult children as successor trustees. If yours is a close-knit family and your final instructions are not of complex longevity, such adult children over eighteen can be your very best bet. You can name one child as sole successor trustee and then list in the order of preference, depending on abilities and/or geographical advantage, which of the others you would have serve as alternates. Or, what often seems to be a better arrangement when your children are few in number and live reasonably close by, you can name them all as co-successor trustees. You would then be required to determine in the trust contract as to whether any necessary decisions on the part of your co-successor trustees would have to be made by majority or unanimous vote.

*Friendship and money: oil and water.*

—MARIO PUZO

Never mind that there has been a bit of sibling bickering over the years. It is a rare family that does not have a spot of altercation going on. However, because your children are usually the contingent beneficiaries, such a nomination forces them to work together and compromise for their own common good. You must be the final judge as to whether or not your children have what it takes to rise to the occasion. Because you have chosen a living trust rather than a will, you have a leg up on any disrupting family squabble. A will is an open invitation to family belligerence and challenge. Almost anyone can contest a will on the weakest of grounds. However, as I pointed out in an earlier chapter, a trust is not only next-to-impossible to dispute, the successor trustees have sovereign control and as long as they follow the rules found in the trust contract, the discontentment registered by the other beneficiaries is a waste of their breath.

Regardless of whom you select as your successor trustee, plug her in to what you are doing. Don't wait to have the undertaker or family accountant spring it on her as a big surprise. You can't conscript her; she has a right to refuse. Talk it over with her, ask for her blessing, and explain how she will be compensated (or why she won't). Show her a copy of your proposed living trust document. Acquaint her with her duties—especially your final instructions to be carried out after your death. Too often unenlightened successor trustees run straight to an attorney to settle the trust, a move that will render all of your trust-

> ### SUCCESSOR TRUSTEE QUALIFICATIONS
>
> ▸ Honesty                   ▸ Strong character
> ▸ Trustworthiness           ▸ Cooperativeness
> ▸ Leadership abilities      ▸ Philosophically compatible with grantor
> ▸ Management abilities      ▸ Proximity of residence
> ▸ Loyalty                   ▸ Understanding of role

making efforts nearly worthless. Keep her informed of major changes you make in your affairs or in your living trust. Your successor trustee has generously and graciously agreed to stand in as watchdog over matters that will have a direct bearing on the welfare of your loved ones when you are gone. You owe your successor trustee all the assistance you can give her while you are physically, mentally, and mortally able.

## CHOOSING YOUR CONTINGENT BENEFICIARIES

Before we get too deeply into the topic of contingent beneficiaries let me define the terms *primary beneficiary* and *contingent beneficiary*. The government says that in a revocable living trust, the grantor of the trust is entitled to every cent the trust earns and thus is not only referred to as both grantor and trustee, but also as the primary beneficiary. Most people assume that the grantor is entitled to all the profits of the trust for whatever reason, so the term primary beneficiary is rarely used or heard. The contingent beneficiaries are those persons that will receive the assets and benefits of the trust *after* the grantor of the trust is dead. The term contingent beneficiary is also rarely used or heard. Most people just refer to them as the *beneficiaries*. There is a difference, however, and you should be able to understand that difference on those rare occasions when the two terms are used.

At first, contingent beneficiaries seem easy enough to choose. "I can pencil those in quickly," you say. But it is a tad more complicated than you first might imagine. Today it is easy; tomorrow, or twenty years from tomorrow, things might be entirely different.

After the surviving spouse dies, chances are that everything will go to your children. Let's call them Peter, Paul, and Mary. But what about the alma mater? Perhaps you would like to leave something to your church or to the Salvation Army. The local Boy Scout troop may be your favorite charity and you might want to outfit them with two or three new tents.

Perhaps Mary is under the age of eighteen and can't inherit on her own. It may be that one or more of your children is impaired or even institutionalized and receives special help and government funds. There may be others that depend on your support such as a parent or in-law.

And what if they all make it safely and happily to adulthood with families of their own, only to lose Peter through accidental death which leaves his wife a widow and his children fatherless? How might this affect Peter's inheritance?

You may have reasons for wanting to divide your estate among your children in unequal shares or even disinherit one of them altogether.

Your diamond ring may be a family heirloom that customarily is handed down to the first-born of the next generation. That original Monet in the dining room has been virtually ignored by your own children, but a favorite niece would give her very soul to own it.

Perhaps a dear friend has unselfishly provided you with a service or comfort for years and you would want him to be remembered.

Your household furnishings and personal possessions may be of unusual beauty or value and to leave them in vague "three equal shares" to your children would invite nothing but a family squabble degenerating into an auction or estate sale out on the front lawn. Would you be content in the hereafter knowing that your treasured solid cherry dining room furniture was peddled to the highest bidder who had designs on painting it barn red and stashing it in her basement rec room?

Indeed, selecting one's beneficiaries and the portions of your possessions to be divided among them is not a spur-of-the-moment decision. It is instead a vital and intricate resolution that can greatly affect the future execution of your personally styled living trust.

Your wishes and those of your spouse are easily incorporated into your trust declaration, but first you must take the time to explore your individual desires and reach a satisfactory agreement between the two of you.

*Money is better than poverty, if only for financial reasons.*

—WOODY ALLEN

## DETERMINING BEQUESTS

Bequests to children, relatives, and friends whom you have chosen to remember with substantial inheritances should be expressed in either percentages or shares (equal or unequal as you wish). However, you may choose to leave a specific asset to a specific person such as "the residence at 405 South St. Johns Street in Niles, Illinois, to Mary Alice, our daughter" and "the Lake Superior log cabin, Lot 7781, Grand Maris, Michigan, to Andrew Craig, our son." These are known as *whole assets* or *undivided assets*.

---

### Smaller Bequests

Exceptions to the rule of naming percentages or shares often apply to smaller gifts of no more than $500 or $1,000. Even in leaner, darker days such trivial amounts should not upset the applecart too badly. Leaving .0025 percent to little Rodney up the street for faithfully walking your dog twice a week for five years is a bit too dispassionate and businesslike. Rather, a gift of a flat $300 for such thoughtful and steadfast service conveys much better the spirit in which the gift is bestowed, and, should the pickings be less than predicted at distribution time, could hardly raise the ire of major beneficiaries.

---

## Whole Assets vs. Shares

There is usually a temptation to leave whole or undivided assets such as a house, car, cottage, or blue chip stock as an outright gift, attempting to juggle the equities fairly among the children. The practice makes the successor trustee's job of settling the estate easy: he neither has to deed a house to perhaps a half-dozen people nor convert the house to cash via a sale to make exact equal division between all the beneficiaries. This is acceptable with real estate and major investments that you intend to hold for "the long haul" over an extended period of years. However, securities, certificates of deposits, and other assets that are sold and traded with any frequency are best treated as cash. As interest rates, dividends, and capital gains fluctuate and investment goals change, your one-year Certificate of Deposit #229683 on the Iowa National Bank at the time of drawing your living trust may be sold, traded, or rolled over into some other type of investment a dozen times in a twenty-year period. Specific assets left to specific people must be included in the trust document. Converting stocks, bonds, certificates of deposit, or insurance policy proceeds to cash is a quick and simple task for your successor trustee and eliminates the necessity of amending your living trust contract each time you alter your investment portfolio or liquidate a certificate of deposit to cash. Such assets, along with savings and other types of accounts, are the "residue" left to beneficiaries in equal or unequal shares after the long-term investments and real estate have been awarded to specific beneficiaries.

Again I remind you that none of the provisions or beneficiaries of your original common living trust is cast in stone. The trust is completely revocable and amendable and, as grantors, you and your spouse may change it as often as you like so long as you follow recommended and lawful procedures.

## Disabled Dependents

A mentally or physically handicapped daughter, son, or parent may be the recipient of such governmental assistance as Supplemental Security Income (SSI) or Medicaid. Indeed, this outside help may be the pivotal point in their very survival. As cold-hearted as it might seem, government agencies have the right to expropriate the inheritances of such unfortunate people in reimbursement for past monies expended in the care of the impaired person. Thus, it is crucial that such persons be placed in a children's or survivor's trust within the parent's trust to safeguard the funds they receive from the government. The handicapped person can be paid the interest and dividend earned on his inheritance and can be directly reimbursed for legitimate expenses. But paying his principal from his share held in the trust will invite Uncle Sam to cut off all future financial aid from the government.

# SELECTING APPOINTEES FOR AUXILIARY DOCUMENTS

## Choosing your Personal Representative

As previously indicated, a well-designed living trust will include a pour-over will. This is the instrument used after your demise to handle those few minor assets that were inadvertently left out of your living trust. Therefore, another decision for you will be to name someone as personal representative. This individual will handle the possibility of a limited, but necessary probate procedure of that part of your estate left outside the trust.

If you have done a perfect job of transferring assets to the trust and there is absolutely nothing left outside, the personal representative you name will have utterly nothing to do. However, on the chance that something will be left out, you will need to appoint such a person in this supplementary document. Grantors who have named a personal friend, relative, or one of their children as successor trustee often coordinate things by appointing the same person to serve as both successor trustee and personal representative.

Failing to appoint a personal representative for your pour-over will invites the probate judge to elect her own choice, which to your family's vexation may introduce a brand-new nose to meddle in your affairs. In fact, it is a wise idea to appoint an *alternate* personal representative as well. To simplify things, grantors often appoint as the alternate personal representative the same person chosen as alternate successor trustee. However, you are free to make the whole scenario just as complicated as you please by choosing a different person for each and every post.

## Choosing Your Attorney-in-Fact

Yet another appointment to concern yourself with is an attorney-in-fact (sometimes referred to as your agent).

As mentioned in chapter 7, your agent has the power to transfer any belated or forgotten asset into your living trust should you be incapacitated, out of the country, or unavailable. Without this agency, your successor trustee has no authority over your assets outside the trust.

The attorney-in-fact or agent holds your financial power of attorney, or the power to act for you in these matters. Trust grantors are free to select anyone they believe could handle the task, and, like the personal representative of their pour-over will, they often feel that it serves in the best interests of simplicity to appoint the person chosen as successor trustee to also serve as agent.

You will probably want to limit the powers of the attorney-in-fact to the prerogatives of conveying assets into the trust. Because these duties are so limited and the danger of open raids on the estate are nil in contrast to power of attorney documents that give carte blanche to the agent, financial custodians have no problem in honoring the document.

## A Note to Grantors

There is a camouflaged hazard in giving your backup trustee even these limited powers of agency. Too often, grantors who have bestowed such authority on some person to act in their place tend to relax on the oars when it comes to transferring their assets into the trust. Wrapped in such an imaginary security blanket, a laxity sneaks in as the grantors lull themselves into believing that the guy drying the dishes will tidy up any gravy stains missed by the guy who was washing them. Realize that no backup trustee can be expected to be as knowledgeable of your assets as you, especially those that you yourself forgot. There is every chance that she too, will miss that old savings account in the Society Bank in South Bend, Indiana. And keep in mind also that any power of attorney, durable or general, *terminates* at the grantor's death.

Once again, it is your responsibility as grantor to get the titles of your assets transferred into your trust. Don't delay! Don't depend on George to do it. Do not consider your living trust complete until to the best of your knowledge all of your assets are safely registered in the name of the trust.

A word about naming an alternate attorney-in-fact: while such a surrogate agent can be the same person chosen as both backup successor trustee and alternate personal representative, keep in mind that anyone named as an alternate attorney-in-fact is no more than a replacement sitting on the bench awaiting playing time in the instance that your original choice strikes out. Unlike successor trustees and personal representatives where there can be only one (or one defined set of co-appointees that work as a team), it is possible to give unlimited numbers of agencies to as many people as you choose. Realize, however, that should you wish to have several people with equal power to transfer assets to your trust, it will require a separate power of attorney document for each agent.

## Choosing a Patient Advocate

A patient advocate is an agent selected by you in the health care power of attorney to make health care decisions for you should you be physically or mentally incapable of making such decisions for yourself. Though not a part of the trust, the specification of the agent is often outlined in an auxiliary document included with the trust package. (See chapter 7.)

The decision should be made with great care. In most cases a primary and a secondary choice is made and either can make such a decision when that time comes.

In choosing a patient advocate, people often become a bit syrup-headed. Because the advocate's duties can very easily include the decree to give the patient continued life or terminate life support, many folks believe that a decision of this magnitude should be placed before all of their children and thus lovingly nominate co-patient advocates (all of the children). I feel that this is usually a mistake.

It is first necessary to consider what will likely be your physical condition and the emotional condition of your children at such a time. It will not be all sunshine and roses as it was on the day you chose your patient advocate(s). Chances are instead you will be in pain and your children will be distraught. Would you wish to be agonizing in a hospital bed while your children, perhaps in tears, were bartering, bargaining, and begging out in the hall as to whether they should let you go?

I feel that this decision should be left solely in the hands of your two strongest children chosen as your primary and backup patient advocate. Both should have the ability to step up to the plate, and, without bending to the influence of their emotional siblings, weigh the facts, consider your wishes, square their shoulders, and make the call.

I also suggest that the chosen patient advocates not sign their portion of the health care power of attorney until a health care decision is necessary. Should your primary choice immediately sign the document and then later be on a vacation in Hawaii at a crucial time of decision, perhaps with you comatose and requiring emergency surgery, the doctors would be hamstrung. By waiting until such a commitment was necessary, your alternate choice for patient advocate could be summoned to sign the document and then okay the surgery.

## CHOOSING GUARDIANS FOR UNDERAGE CHILDREN

A personal guardian for underage children in the happenstance of the grantor's death more often than not is someone other than that person named in the combined posts of successor trustee, personal representative, and attorney-in-fact. This is due to the fact that attributes and virtues of the guardian are often much different. While your successor trustee, personal representative, or agent is generally chosen for mature judgment in financial matters, the guardian is selected for his ability to rear your children within an atmosphere and value system that you espouse. Thus, the guardian is often a close friend rather than a relative.

When you also specify the spouse of the person you select as guardian ("Mr. and Mrs. Donald Mason") you invite problems. Should the Masons eventually divorce or your actual principal guardian choice, Donald's wife, Susan, die, Donald could conceivably remarry someone whom you would not want parenting your children. Such a possible entanglement is avoided by naming only "Susan Mason" as guardian and then another selection as an alternate personal guardian should Donald and Susan divorce or should Susan die.

## YOUR GRANDCHILDREN

Don't lose track of the fact that even though your children may all be of legal age, in the unfortunate circumstance that one of them dies before you, it may well be that minor-aged children of your deceased child will inherit your child's portion of your trust. In such a case, to avoid involving probate court in their lives, you must make sure that their inheritance is held in the safekeeping of your trust until they are of legal age.

These are the types of contingencies for which attorneys love to prepare. Anything they can cram into the trust document will add to its length and jack up their fee. What if one of your children dies before you? What if your child divorces, remarries a widow, and you inherit three new grandchildren? What if you die on a day when the sun comes up in the west? Anything an attorney can add between the handsome, leather-bound covers of the trust adds to the fee.

Most such calamities will not suddenly come at you out of the blue. Remember that should one of your children precede you in death you will still be alive to amend and revamp your trust contract. At that time you can amend your trust and set up a children's trust for any underage grandchildren and prevent the management of their inheritances from being taken over by probate court.

If you wish, children's trusts and other protective provisions within your trust contract can be set up from day one. In fact, your trust contract can include page after page of remedies for unlikely future events that have only a measly chance of ever happening. Attorneys relish this opportunity because it adds many more pages to the trust contract for which they can charge. Because such remote experiences will probably never come to pass, it is better to cross those bridges when you come to them by amending your trust contract to take care of such offbeat episodes. Cluttering up your trust contract with safeguards to problems that have only a minute chance of materializing does little more than add great confusion for your successor trustee at the time of settling the trust. In such cases, even successor trustees familiar with your trust contract and your affairs must often spend days searching through page after page of legal mumbo jumbo to make sure that they have not missed some tiny, but important detail. Again, the simpler your trust contract, the better the trust you have.

# 9

# From One Pocket to Another

Regardless of what you have been told by friends, relatives, or an attorney, listing your assets in a schedule or memorandum within the Declaration of Trust document has no legal merit and will not get the job done. The title to each of your assets must be registered in a manner that reflects ownership by the trust rather than you. All assets left outside of your trust (not re-titled) must endure the probate procedure. Those stray assets will then be placed within your trust by the court, providing that you have executed a pour-over will that bequeaths all such assets to your trust as sole heir. Therefore, it will save your heirs time and money if you re-title your assets in the name of your living trust during your lifetime.

## ALLOW THE FINANCIAL CUSTODIANS TO DO THE JOB

In the beginning you should understand that with proper organization, the current financial custodians of your assets will be happy to transfer your assets to the trust. You need only contact them and make your wants known. Regardless of what an attorney has told you about some imagined difficulty in transferring assets to the trust, the procedure is exactly the same that you went through to open your checking account.

It takes no more than fifteen minutes. In reality you are simply taking your assets out of one pocket and putting them in another.

In regard to your financial custodians, keep in mind that you are their customer. You are not working for them; they are working for you. That puts you in the driver's seat. They make money only when their customers are happy with the services they provide. You may run into a grumpy and unobliging registrar of deeds at the courthouse who has to face the voters only once every four years to ensure his job. However, it is the business of progressive financial custodians such as banks, stockbrokers, and insurance agents in a competitive market to bend over backward to be of service to their customers. Should any one of them display an attitude that suggests you are an interruption to their work, you have every right to take your business elsewhere.

Having decided on a name for your trust, the first hard rule of successful transferring is to make sure that you always register both old and new assets *exactly* as the name of your trust appears on your trust declaration document. The same is true of your personal signature. Form the habit of always using the same signature format—not "John R. Jones" on one document and "J. R. Jones" on another. Because the official trust name is not in everyday use and is often lengthy, it is wise to write or type the official trust name on a piece of paper and carry it with you at all times in your wallet or purse. Remember, any major purchase you make (house, car, boat, refrigerator, or TV) where a receipt, bill of sale, or deed is given should be made in the name of your living trust. This will avoid any possible future misunderstanding or argument.

Though an official list of assets within your actual Declaration of Trust document is not required, you should strongly consider stapling or clipping to your trust contract an informal record of your assets and the location of the titles to such assets.

### Asset Titles That Name Beneficiaries

The exceptions to this rule of transferring all assets to the trust are assets for which you can name a *Payment-on-Death* (P.O.D.) or *Transfer-on-Death* (T.O.D.) beneficiary directly on the asset title (discussed in chapter 1). In many states this would include life insurance policies, annuities, IRA-type accounts, most stocks and mutual funds, checking accounts, savings accounts, money market accounts, and certificates of deposit.

Your insurance policies, annuities, and IRA-type accounts undoubtedly already list a beneficiary. If the bank accounts, certificates of deposit, stocks, and mutual funds listed above do not already name a P.O.D. or T.O.D. beneficiary, there is scant value in adding such a beneficiary at this time. It is just as easy to place those accounts within your living trust in order to name a beneficiary to an already existing private account.

If you have already named individuals as P.O.D. beneficiaries on your various bank accounts and CDs, you may want to consider changing those beneficiaries to the name of your trust. In so doing, final distribution of all your assets is then made under the umbrella of your living trust, and your successor trustee will have complete control and may be able to do a more equitable job of distributing your assets. Be sure to inform your successor trustee of any assets passing to heirs outside of your trust, on the chance that your trust could be affected by such a transfer.

## TRANSFERRING MOTOR VEHICLES

Automobiles come under heavy use and depreciate rapidly; most people own many during their lifetime. To cut down on what would be a mountain of paperwork caused by the constant buying, trading, selling, and registering of autos, the vehicle code of every state now exempts most motor vehicles from the probate code. In other words, your car does not require probate. (Some states limit the amount of vehicles that may be transferred without probate.) Simply take the car title and death certificate to your Secretary of State's office (license bureau) and ask them to make the change. This usually only takes a few minutes.

Nonetheless, it is judicious to keep all assets—even those that avoid probate and still pass to heirs outside of your trust—under the umbrella of your living trust. In so doing, you make your successor trustee's job of transferring assets to the beneficiaries more uniform. While there is no need to rush down to the Secretary of State's office to transfer your present vehicles into the name of your trust, you should strongly consider registering all future vehicles purchased by you in the name of the trust. This is done simply by instructing the auto salesman to register the vehicle you are purchasing in the official name of your trust.

## TRANSFERRING GENERAL ACCOUNTS

The transferring of savings accounts, checking accounts, money market accounts, certificates of deposit, treasury bills, Ginnie Maes, and credit union accounts can be initiated with either a letter of transfer, a personal face-to-face visit, or a telephone call.

Your financial custodians will require your official authority to execute a transfer of your assets into your trust that at some point will require your personal signature on financial custodian-provided forms. The manner in which you initiate the transfer will depend largely on your own personal convenience, the geographic location of the financial custodian, and your personal relationship with the personnel at your financial custodian's offices.

More often than not, trust grantors are on a first-name basis with a financial custodian's staff. Such familiarity facilitates a simple telephone call or a "drop by" type of personal visit. Alternatively, much, if not all, of the information required can be conveyed by phone. The transfer papers can either be mailed to the trust grantor for signature or the trust grantor can drop by the custodian's offices at a convenient time and sign the papers there. In cases where your relationship with your financial custodian is on a more formal basis, you may find it better to initiate the transfer with a "letter of transfer," a sample of which appears at the end of this chapter.

All in all, the face-to-face visit is the most efficient approach and will almost always get the entire task completed in a five- to fifteen-minute conference with near zero chance of foul-ups and misunderstandings. Questions can be asked directly when they arise, rather than trying to communicate by mail, or through impersonal faxes or online communication.

---

**Letters of Transfer**

If for some reason the financial custodian cannot complete the job on the spot, it is wise to follow up with a phone call or letter a day or two later that lends an official tone to your desires and lets the financial custodian know that you expect your request to be expediently carried out in a business-like manner. A letter of transfer should be followed up with a telephone call within seventy-two hours.

A letter of transfer will trigger the custodian to forward to you its own forms used for such transfers. Usually such forms arrive completely filled out and require only your signature. On the other hand, the representative may invite you to stop by at a predetermined time to sign the papers in her office.

---

## Your Personal Checking Account

A checking account in the name of a trust is sometimes a little awkward. If you are married, most of your trust assets will require both signatures to sell them or cash them in. This of course does not work very well on a checking account. However, if you promise yourself to keep the balance low (no more than $3,000 to $5,000), your bank will most likely transfer the personal checking account to the surviving spouse immediately upon death. This is generally not an arrangement that a bank will put in writing. However, in almost every case banks will turn over small amounts of cash (especially to a surviving spouse) without the fear of being sued by some disgruntled heir. (This is most likely because the cost of hiring an attorney and suing would in all

## Automatic Teller Machines

If you now have or are considering "after-hours" automatic teller machine (ATM) service that requires a bank-issued credit card to make withdrawals, you should know that few banks will permit such an account to be held in the name of a trust. There are several ways around this, but the easiest by far is to leave any of your checking accounts that include the added ATM feature outside of your trust. By naming your living trust as the P.O.D. beneficiary on your checking account(s), rather than attempting to have your bank re-title them in the name of the trust, the balance in the account will avoid probate and, upon your death, automatically flow into your living trust and be subject to the distribution schedule provided by the trust.

probability exceed the amount the heir would have received had she won the suit.)

If you do choose to place your checking account in your trust, you may be able to keep the same account number, which will negate the need to order new checks. Also, you should know that regardless of what the bank officer tells you, it is not necessary to replace your own printed name on your personal checks with the name of your trust. Keeping your own name on your printed checks as opposed to replacing it with the name of your trust often cuts confusion when using checks at a convenience store or gas station and thus it is important to stick to your guns on this. Feel not a qualm about going over the bank officer's head to a higher authority, if necessary.

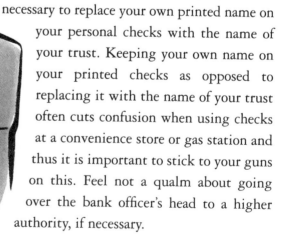

## Safety Deposit Boxes

It is advantageous to also place your safety deposit box in the name of your trust. A few banks still cling to the archaic practice of sealing the box at death until such time as the state can inspect the contents. Generally, a joint tenant or P.O.D. beneficiary listed on bank records has access to the box. Registering the box in the name of the trust does away with any doubts because the trustee(s) and, later, the successor trustee, has access to the box at any time. Ask your bank to make this safety deposit box change of record at the same time they are re-titling your accounts.

# STOCKS, BONDS, AND MUTUAL FUNDS

Your stockbroker is well versed in the mechanics of re-titling your securities and it is sagacious to place yourself directly in his hands.

Because most stockbrokers and their representatives do their utmost to keep their relationships with their customers informal, it is best to set up an appointment for a face-to-face meeting with your investment banker and, with a copy of your living trust document in hand, explain directly what you wish to do.

Generally, stockbrokers are most astute in the matter of finance. They are anxious to be of service and will quickly pick up the ball and run with it. Understand, however, that many brokerage houses have recently gone into the trust managing business in competition with commercial banks. Thus, you may experience a bit of pressure from your account executive to name his employer as your trustee.

Understand, too, that while brokerage houses are well versed in the mechanics of transferring assets into a trust, and many are now vying to be named trustee, there are still many brokers that do not understand the philosophy of the trust. Such stockbrokers succumb to the same legal profession intimidation that paralyzes the general public. Because they require a charter to do business, they are deathly afraid that anything that smacks of practicing law without a license might lead to the loss of their charter to deal in stocks and bonds.

Consequently, out of fear of rocking their boat, stockbrokers are often among the legal profession's greatest allies, parroting the propaganda of attorneys at every opportunity. When you finish this book, however, you will understand a great deal more about trusts and the philosophy of your trust than does your stockbroker.

## Street Name Accounts

If your holdings are in the currently popular "street name" type of account, the transfer procedure will be simple. In a street name account, your stocks and bonds are registered in the name of the stockbroker. In turn the stockbroker issues a receipt to you (the stockholder) indicating the number of shares you own in various corporations. A statement is issued to you every month or quarter regarding your investment portfolio performance. The rationale behind this is the same as the bank's, which does not write your name on every one hundred dollar bill you deposit to make sure that you get the same bill back. Instead, your end-of-the-month (or quarter) statement reflects all aspects of how your investments are doing. Like one hundred dollar bills, all shares of General Motors stock (or any other company's stock) are identical and treated alike; one share is as good as the next. Such transfers of your shares to the name of the trust is as simple as transferring your cash at the bank into the trust. Simply make the request of your stockbroker and, upon their approval of your trust contract, the transfer will usually be made while you wait.

## Individually Held Stock Certificates

The alternative to a street name account is to own securities in your own name and have personal possession of the stock certificates issued directly by the corporation in which the stock is owned. In most such cases your stockbroker will also assist you in the transferring of such stocks, usually at no charge if your broker values you as a customer. If you do not have a stockbroker, it will be necessary for you to obtain an irrevocable stock or bond power form (refer to the sample form in

Appendix B) from any brokerage firm or full-service bank. It is necessary that you sign your name to this instrument *exactly* as it appears on the face of the stock or bond, have your signature guaranteed by the bank or a recognized stock exchange–listed brokerage house, and then forward the instrument and the stock certificate to the transfer agent whose name appears on the certificate.

> ### A Word of Caution
> Stock certificates and bonds remain non-negotiable as long as they are unsigned. Once signed or placed in the same hands together with the signed stock or bond power form, they become immediately negotiable by anyone! Thus, it is wise to forward the *unsigned* stock certificate or bond via a separate certified mailing envelope from the stock or bond power form. Only when the two envelopes arrive at the transfer agent's office will the two documents be joined together and the stock certificate become negotiable.

Should you have even a "part time" stockbroker, this entire procedure of transferring personally held stock certificates can often be negated. Simply ask the broker to do it for you. Never mind the fact that she did not sell you the stock. The brokerage business is highly competitive and most brokers will honor your request rather than risk your visiting the stockbroker down on the third floor and requesting that they do it. (After all, you might decide to stay and partake of more of their services.)

A strong inducement for having your individually held stock certificates converted into a street name account at your brokerage house is the fact that, upon death, only one death certificate will be required by your successor trustee to have your entire investment portfolio transferred to your designated beneficiaries. Otherwise, if the stockholder has possession of his own individual stock certificates, a separate death certificate will be required for each corporation in which stock is held.

# INSURANCE POLICIES, RETIREMENT, AND PENSION PLANS

Life insurance, annuities, ESOPs, IRAs, Keogh plans, pension plans, and profit-sharing plans almost always name a beneficiary. That is to say, when death occurs, the proceeds from that insurance policy or retirement plan will avoid probate and flow immediately to whomever you have named on the title (policy) as the beneficiary.

## If You Are Married

The one danger in naming your spouse as the beneficiary is that should the two of you die simultaneously or within one hundred twenty hours of each other (perhaps as the result of the same accident), the proceeds will have to endure the ordeal of probate, with the legal system biting a large chunk out of funds that you thought you had sheltered from probate.

By naming your living trust as the primary beneficiary of your life insurance, you assure that the proceeds from the policy will directly and immediately flow into your trust and become subject to the distribution schedule outlined in your living trust; there is absolutely no way that probate can become involved.

An alternative is to name your spouse as beneficiary of your life insurance and add your living trust as *contingent beneficiary.* Thus, if the spouses die coincidently, the proceeds will flow directly to the trust rather than through probate court.

With IRAs and other retirement funds, the alternative plan of naming your trust as a contingent beneficiary is actually preferred. The government's recent approval of permitting an IRA to be owned by a trust is fairly new and there is always the chance that some inexperienced clerk could err in such a transfer and trigger a distribution that would be costly tax-wise. I would venture that it is safer simply to name the trust as a contingent beneficiary. Thus, on retirement accounts it is proper and prudent to name your spouse as primary beneficiary and your living trust as contingent beneficiary.

## If You Are Single

All insurance policies, retirement plans, and accounts that carry a beneficiary should name the trust as primary beneficiary. The funds then flow directly to the trust and are distributed according to terms of the trust. Then there is no danger of a beneficiary perishing with you, sending the funds to probate court in search of a new beneficiary.

Whether married or single, it is not necessary to name a contingent beneficiary on insurance policies if you have named your living trust as primary beneficiary.

## Transfer of Ownership

If you anticipate your life insurance to accumulate to substantial cash value, you may want to consider the transfer of the actual ownership of the policy into the name of the trust (the owner is usually the person that pays the premiums). When your living trust is the owner of the policy—as well as being its primary beneficiary—your successor trustee, having the power to step in and manage the trust upon your incapacity, can borrow funds against the policy to be used for your care. Until recently, the actual transfer of ownership of a retirement account such as an IRA triggered what the IRS considered a *distribution,* making you immediately liable for the taxes on the sheltered principal and any earnings acquired by the fund since its inception. However, because of the living trust's rapidly increasing popularity, the IRS has relaxed this rule and allowed such an account to be actually owned by the trust.

Again, because you are a valued customer of your life insurance underwriter and the insurance company he represents, one or the other should be most happy to assist you. First, contact your agent (by telephone if you prefer) and explain that you want to either change your insurance beneficiary to the name of your trust or add your trust as a contingent beneficiary. In a matter of a day or two, he should be able to provide you with the proper forms and instructions relative to the company that holds your policy. Should your agent be located close by, you might want simply to stop by his office. If the agent is located in a different community, you may be able to handle the entire process by mail or fax.

The custodian of an employer-initiated IRA or other retirement-type account is often a bank or financial institution in a different city or even a different state. To inquire about their procedure, it might be wise to start with a telephone call directly to the name or phone number appearing on your periodic account statement. Most likely they will request that you mail or fax them a written statement of your intentions, whereupon they will return the proper forms to you along with instructions on how to complete them. The entire process should be completed in ten days to two weeks.

At the end of this chapter, you will find a sample letter to be written to IRA-type custodians as a follow-up to your telephone inquiry or response to their request for an official written notification.

## HOUSEHOLD AND PERSONAL POSSESSIONS

Many living trust documents contain a cumbersome schedule of assets on which to list the grantor's titled and untitled assets as well as real estate. Over the years such a schedule is very difficult to keep current. As previously mentioned, this list is entirely unnecessary except in cases where co-grantors wish to maintain separately designated assets within the trust.

It cannot be emphasized too strongly that assets that have been re-titled in the name of the trust *automatically* become a part of the trust estate. Houses, bank accounts, stock certificates, and any other assets that have not been re-titled in the name of the trust are not a part of the trust; to simply include them on some schedule within the trust document is an exercise in futility.

However, everyone owns many household items for which there are no written titles other than long-lost cash register receipts or purchase agreements. It is customary that the contents of a piece of real estate transfer to the new owner right along with the real estate unless otherwise noted. However "custom" is not quite safe enough. Thus, a short auxiliary document known as a *bill of sale* (see Appendix B for a sample) can be used to sweep all such items located at your various real properties or other locales into the trust.

All living trust packages purchased from the National Center for the Avoidance of Probate include a bill of sale for household assets. This bill of sale lists each location where personal property is held: home, cottage at the lake, Florida condo, business office, banks where you rent safety deposit boxes, and so forth.

Also, give some thought to any personal assets (machinery, tools, musical instruments, art treasures, and other similar items) that might be on loan to a friend, relative, church, school, or lodge. To avoid any misunderstanding between your successor trustee and the custodians of such possessions, all such possessions should be appended in the space provided for such additional personal property.

The bill of sale need not be notarized, but should carry your signature as both grantor and trustee and should be stapled to the last page of your trust contract.

# BUSINESS INTERESTS

## Sole Proprietorship and Partnership

Should you be the sole proprietor of a business or service, you should have each of your business licenses and permits changed to show that your living trust is now the owner. Should you be registered with your county as doing business under an assumed name (DBA) such as Sunny Side Cafe or High Flyer Aviation, you should change this "Doing Business As" to reflect that the business is owned by your trust.

There are, of course, many different federal, state, county, and local agencies that issue various licenses and permits under which a firm does business—each with its own rules, regulations, and methods. In the interest of expediency, a simple telephone call to those involved will inform you of the steps required by each and whether the required changes can be effected via telephone, mail, e-mail, fax, or through the agency's Web site—or whether a personal visit by you will be necessary.

The matter should also be discussed with your bank. If your business accounts are listed as being actually owned by you, you will want them changed to indicate that they are owned by the trust. To transfer a privately owned corporation, you can void the stock certificates issued to you and replace them with new certificates indicating the owner to be your trust. Generally, you can find blank stock certificates in your corporation minutes book.

When changing a partnership in a business from your own name to that of your trust, it is best to start out by reviewing the by-laws of the partnership and discussing your intentions with the other partners. The transfer can be made through a bill of sale in which the trust purchases your personal interest in the business.

## Limited Partnerships

Limited partnerships vary and there is no way to give you explicit directions as to how to transfer into your trust those in which you have an interest. In most cases, the general partners will handle this matter for you. You need only contact them. I recommend that you follow the procedure of an official letter of transfer (similar to that used for banks) with a follow-up telephone call within a week.

## TRANSFERRING REGISTERED ASSETS INTO THE TRUST

Real estate, mortgages, or notes that are *owed to you* are somewhat unique. They are among the few assets that are in your "possession" as opposed to being held by a financial custodian. However, because such assets are almost always registered with the county registrar of deeds office, you will need to execute deeds and assignments that transfer such items to your trust.

## Placing Real Estate into the Trust

To place real estate into your trust, you will need to transfer the title of each parcel of real estate—don't forget business real estate—that you presently own *exactly* as it appears on the deed that you received when you acquired the property. That means the legal description on the deed that you give to the trustees must match exactly that of the deed that conveyed the property to you, and that you transfer the property under the same name that you received it. If you purchased the property as John Barry Smith, you must transfer the property as John Barry Smith, not John B. Smith.

A warranty deed can be used but is not required. You are not selling such property; you are only correcting the name of the property's owner on the county records. A warranty deed guarantees that the property is yours to sell, and will require expensive title searches or title insurance. You are merely taking the property from one pocket and putting it in the other, so there is no need to guarantee that the property is yours as you would have to do if you were transferring it to a different individual. Thus, an inexpensive quitclaim deed will nicely do the job for you. (See Appendix B for an example of a quitclaim deed.)

Under normal conditions, the transfer of real estate into your living trust will incur the lion's share of the expense of the entire process of transferring assets into the trust. It entails a fee for every deed you transfer. The fee ranges from seven dollars to fifteen dollars depending on the state in which you live. The fee is set by the legislature in some states and by the county in others.

Many people run for the safety of an attorney when transferring real estate, and most attorneys are happy to oblige, charging one hundred to two hundred dollars to do the simple paperwork involved in transferring each deed. However, the job is no more difficult than any other trust-creating task. Quitclaim deeds as well as assignment forms are very self-explanatory. Trust makers can purchase such forms at office supply stores and stationery stores for just a few dollars or purchase software that will make simple quitclaim deeds on the family computer. Keep in mind, however, that absolute accuracy is required. Thus, take plenty of time and utilize extra patience when filling in the legal description of the property just as it appears on your present deed.

Your county registrar of deeds office requires that the document be both witnessed and notarized and that the names of the witnesses and notary public be typed or printed below their signatures. You are also required to note that you prepared the document privately.

> *Money is of no value; it cannot spend itself. All depends on the skill of the spender.*
>
> —Ralph Waldo Emerson

## Placing Mortgages and Contracts Owed to Grantor in the Trust

Debts of a substantial nature *owed to you* and secured by a mortgage, note, or contract are usually registered at the county registrar of deeds office to prevent the debtor from selling the property without notifying his buyer that a lien is owed on the property.

If you hold such a mortgage, note, or contract, you can choose to 1) ask your debtor to sign a new note indicating that the money is owed to your living trust rather than to you (then destroy the old agreement) or, if you believe that the debtor would be uncooperative, 2) personally assign the credit to your living trust with an assignment form (see Appendix B for an example of such a form).

Like the quitclaim deed, simple assignment forms are usually available at office supply stores for two or three dollars each. In fact, for just a few dollars more, software containing many simple forms such as quitclaim deeds, assignment forms, rental agreements, and eviction notices is now available and may expedite this entire process.

**Sample letter of transfer for savings accounts, checking accounts, and certificates of deposit**

Smithtown Community Bank
1234 Michigan Avenue
Smithtown, Michigan 49ZIP

RE: Certificate of Deposit #54321
    Saving Account #98765
    Checking Account #121212

We are currently registering our assets in the name of our living trust.

Please re-title Certificate of Deposit and Saving accounts listed above in the following name:

> The James & Jean Jones Family Trust
> James Jones and Jean Jones, trustees,
> under date of trust (UDT) 3/12/89

In regard to our joint checking account, we wish it to remain in our private ownership. However we wish to add the above named trust as beneficiary to be paid upon the death of the surviving spouse.

Kindly advise us of any new account numbers assigned. We can be reached at the following telephone numbers:

> Home (616) 222-3333
> Business (616) 333-4444

Thank you.

_____
*(signature)*
James Jones, transferor

_____
*(signature)*
Jean Jones, transferor

_____
*(signature)*
James Jones, transferee

_____
*(signature)*
Jean Jones, transferee

## Sample written follow-up to your in-person request for transfer of assets

Mr. (name of bank officer)
Smithtown Community Bank
1234 Michigan Avenue
Smithtown, Michigan 49ZIP

RE: Change of account names

Dear (bank officer):

On March 29 we visited with you in your office, requesting that the names of the following accounts be registered in the name of our trust:

Certificate of Deposit    #54321
Savings Account    #98765

In the future these accounts should reflect ownership by our living trust named as follows:

The James & Jean Jones Family Trust
James Jones and Jean Jones, trustees
under date of trust (UDT) 3/12/89

In regard to joint checking account #121212, we have elected to keep this account in our personal names. However, we wish to add the above named trust as beneficiary payable upon the death of the surviving spouse.

We are relying on you to accurately make these account name changes as soon as possible and it is our assumption that there will be no charge for this service. Please notify us when you have completed these changes.

Thank you.

_(signature)_
_____
James Jones

_(signature)_
_____
Jean Jones

## Sample written request for addition of a contingent beneficiary

Ms. Mae Barton
National Bank of Chicago
12554 Sears Tower
Chicago, Illinois 60ZIP

Re: Account #2200790
    Addition of contingent beneficiary

Ms. Barton:

As per our telephone conversation of November 18, please consider this to be my formal request to add the name of my living trust as contingent beneficiary of the above named IRA account.

My trust is titled:
The Matthew Martin Trust, Matthew B. Martin, trustee, UDT 10/24/89.

Please forward all necessary forms and instructions to me at my home address: 2209 Badger Avenue, Ludington, Michigan 49ZIP.

In no way should this request be construed as a request for distribution of the fund. I request only the addition of a contingent beneficiary.

Yours truly,


(signature)
Matthew B. Martin

# 10

# Final Decisions

I am often accused of being hard on both the attorneys and the legal profession. This did not come about by accident; I intend to be! The legal profession, though undeniably a community necessity, has a monopolistic and vice-like grip on society. Since its establishment as we know it during the Roman Empire, it has been allowed to write its own rules, dictate its own code of ethics and, where criminal law has not been violated, ride herd on its own constituents through its own state and national associations. History records that such self-discipline leaves a great deal to be desired.

It has been obvious for years that because members of the legal profession pass judgment on both themselves and those who challenge them, a classic conflict of interest exists. Consequently, the legal profession's policing of their own for fifteen hundred years has resulted in the reputation of a craft that has a license to steal and that stands on the integrity scale comparable to a street corner shell game.

John Q. Public perceives that legal fees and greed have been allowed to go over the moon while ethics have been allowed to go under the rug. Just as with health care, many Americans in the lower income brackets avoid legal help out of fear of the cost. Many folks with little more than legal sore throats shy away from even telephoning an attorney. They are afraid that their desire to get the answers to one or two simple questions will result either in a cold demand from the attorney to make an appointment or a one hundred dollar charge in the morning mail for a "telephone conference."

During his tenure as vice-president, Dan Quayle ascribed many of the nation's insurance and medical cost ills to rapacious tort lawyers seeking multi-million dollar settlements that drive up the cost of everything from a tonsillectomy to a trail bike. However, in spite of the fact that juries today are awarding millions of dollars of other people's money to injured parties, most Americans manage to make it through life without even getting scratched. Though murder and mayhem in our streets have become almost as common as double-parked delivery trucks, the overwhelming majority of the citizenry rarely gets closer to the long arm of the law than the twenty minutes required every few years to renew their driver's licenses. Other than for jury duty, most Americans have never been inside a courtroom.

Most of the billions of dollars in fees annually plucked from the American public by the legal profession result not from headline-grabbing, multi-million dollar lawsuits, but rather from the humdrum proceedings of divorce, evictions, property transfer, custody wars, dog bites, drunk driving, bankruptcy, and probate—all squeezed from the public pocket by the friendly family attorney with modest offices on the second floor of the community bank building. Attorneys' near-exclusive license to perform such minuscule and mundane services as rental agreements, collections, and transferal of real estate is protected the way a hound guards a ham bone.

With the help of the American Bar Association and state bars, attorneys have literally invented both their profession and their practice. The craft has become masked in mystique, intimidation, and the dead language of Latin. And because the nation's law schools are currently generating 75,000 new attorneys each year, the ability to "make work" is now the key to success in nearly every law office.

The preventive medicine practiced and promoted today by the medical and dental professions is almost nonexistent in the legal profession. The same judges and attorneys who chortle that ignorance of the law is no excuse do precious little to put an end to legal illiteracy. They have in many states even successfully outlawed self-written holographic wills, and, where that has failed, enjoyed some success in

*People are getting smarter nowadays; they are letting lawyers, instead of their conscience, be their guide.*

—WILL ROGERS

coercing local notaries public into refusing to attest to the signatures of witnesses on such self-drawn wills.

In Florida, an attorney manipulated a five-month jail sentence for his secretary when he learned that she was drawing divorce papers at twenty-five dollars each for destitute couples that could not afford the services of her boss.

In Connecticut, an entire state bar association and its members came down on non-attorney Norman Dacey, who dared to spread the good news throughout New England and New York that it was legal, ethical, and easy to design your own living trust.

Thus, who will hold the feet of the friendly family lawyer to the fire? And, would it do any good? Are there any honest lawyers left in the country?

To the latter question I can answer yes—some by nature and the rest by holding their feet to the fire. That's what this final chapter is all about: how to protect your interests and receive honest service from your attorney, should you choose to hire one to plan your estate.

## IF YOU CHOOSE TO HAVE AN ATTORNEY DRAW YOUR TRUST

After twelve years of assisting Americans from every state in the union with their estate planning and cataloging more than three thousand direct complaints against attorneys in this field, I am convinced that ninety-five percent of the public will end up with a better trust if they do it themselves. However, if you choose to have an attorney draw your living trust, I want you to get a fair shake. The key to such a happening is to gain the attorney's respect by being as well informed as possible when you walk through her office door.

## Six Important Points to Remember When Consulting an Attorney

1. *Evaluate your motivations:* First and foremost, you should be visiting an attorney's office only because there are unusual circumstances in your financial life that prevent you from creating your own trust.

2. *Don't let the attorney intimidate you:* Keep in mind throughout your conferences with the attorney that just like sitting down to a family dinner, the settling of a living trust is meant to be a private affair. If you want to devour the apple pie before you eat the chicken noodle soup you don't need your attorney's permission or that of the cop down on the corner. It is strictly your business. As a matter of fact, your selection of a successor trustee is much more important than your selection of an attorney, and, should the attorney attempt to frighten you with terrifying consequences from not abiding by his sacred word, you should point this fact out to him.

3. *Arrive prepared:* Many attorneys spend the first few minutes of an initial conference measuring the gullibility and the financial means of the client seated on the other side of the desk. The first word a newborn attorney learns is *retainer,* and if the client won't agree to such an up-front bond, the attorney will set about to organize the client's affairs in a manner that will turn that client into a regular customer.

   That does not mean that you should immediately get into a wits-matching contest with a glib attorney; you would likely lose, hands down. However, wearing your heart on your sleeve gives off a signal that you are a candidate for lifelong assistance.

   Actually, it is just the other way around; you are there to measure the attorney! You do so by arming yourself with as much understanding and knowledge of living trusts as you possibly can and then calmly asking questions that will either prove that the attorney is just the person you are looking for or expose her as a rank novice who would like to pick up a few living trust frequent flyer miles on your money. Understand that most attorneys will have less than two hours' time involved in your trust (attorney counseling and secretarial time at the computer). Thus, you must determine what is a fair price for two hours' worth of professional labor.

4. *Evaluate the attorney's experience:* You should inquire of your attorney just how many living trusts he draws in a year's time. If the number is not impressive you don't want him. And if the attorney comes up with an imposing figure, he should then have no problem giving you a package price for the work about to be done for you. Living trusts drawn by experienced trust lawyers are much more generic than the lawyers would like you to believe. They usually have a living trust document poised on their computer just waiting to be merged with the name of a new client.

   You should consider it automatic disqualification if after having inquired about the price, the attorney reverts to rhetoric that each trust is different and that an hourly rate is always charged. What he is telling you is that either he believes you are a dolt or that his lack of experience in trust work will require some boning up at the local law library and he is planning to charge you for his time in research.

> *It is the trade of lawyers to question everything, yield nothing, and to talk by the hour.*
> —THOMAS JEFFERSON

5. *Avoid revealing how much you're worth:* Legal fees mysteriously multiply as the client reveals advanced levels of his wealth. Thus, disclose your financial worth to the attorney at your own peril and certainly only after you have settled on a price for his labors. Unless your financial position puts you close to the altitude at which federal estate taxes kick in, there is absolutely no good reason for telling the attorney what you are worth.

Certainly you will have to give the attorney a picture of what you own. After all, you have come to the attorney because you have special problems that set you apart from the ordinary mainstream trust maker. The attorney cannot advise you on such matters unless you clue him in. From this information his canny mind will certainly draw a reasonable picture of your total worth. However, as you already know, a living trust has no bearing on income taxes; only estate taxes. Thus, your proximity to the estate tax entry level is all the attorney officially needs to know until he commits to a flat fee.

6. *Know what you're getting:* Finally, you should have a complete understanding with your attorney as to what her package price includes. A well-drawn living trust should contain at least the following documents:

- the Declaration of Trust

- pour-over wills for each grantor

- financial powers of attorney for each grantor

- health care powers of attorney for each grantor

In addition to these documents, most living trust designers also include in their package a management file with instructions as to just how the trustee should proceed to transfer assets to the trust and how the successor trustee is to later settle the trust.

It is of the utmost importance that you have a complete understanding of your trust and the language in it. Only then will you be able to make your own changes in the trust as the events of your life unfold and will your successor trustee be able to wrap up your affairs and distribute the assets to the beneficiaries quickly and independently. For these reasons you should demand that along with the trust documents the attorney furnish an abstract that explains in plain English just what is going on in the Latin legalese written in the documents. Under no condition should you allow yourself to be put off by friendly pats on the back and the attorney's pledge that he will take care of everything. That is precisely what you don't want to happen! The entire strategy is to avoid the high cost of probate; you don't want simply to replace it with a high-priced living trust.

## Other Elements of an Attorney-Drawn Living Trust

Most attorney-offered living trust packages also include the transfer of your real estate and any registered debts (mortgages, contracts, and so forth) owed to you into your trust. This is not a difficult job; however, because it does require forms prepared in a predetermined format of which your attorney is familiar, it is probably wise to allow her to proceed with this matter.

Bank and credit union accounts, stocks, bonds, insurance policy beneficiaries, and most other personal properties are a different matter. They are easily transferred into the trust by short personal visits, informal letters, and even an occasional private telephone call. No one knows this better than the attorney, and no one more than your attorney hopes that you don't know it. By convincing you that this task of transferring assets to trust ownership is long and complicated, he hopes to be commissioned with the task, enabling him to double the price of the trust.

Agency power to transfer your assets into a living trust should be handed over to your attorney only if you find yourself totally baffled by the technique of such transfer or if you feel that the personal inconvenience justifies the price.

## THE FUTURE:
## YOURS TO CHOOSE

*Lawyers [are] operators of the toll bridge across which anyone in search of justice has to pass.*

—JANE BRYANT QUINN

Since the beginning of time, death has been the supreme enemy of man. Though we all originated from non-existence, the thought of returning to it is most troublesome—often unthinkable—for many.

We are indebted to millions of professionals for relieving us of our fears and money in regard to our forthcoming demise. By harnessing that fear, the legal craft has held the populace hostage to the probate system for centuries. In their legal store, probate has been one of their more popular shelf items. In fact, today it accounts for nearly twenty percent of the total legal billings in the country.

However, suppressing knowledge is like trying to create a perfect vacuum. No matter how hard the tyrant tries to plug all the holes, a bit of fresh air always penetrates, widening the crack and permitting the passage of even more fresh air.

Now, news is rapidly spreading that there is a simple and easy detour around the tollgate that attorneys have been permitted to erect at the end of life on this planet. No longer is it necessary to pay the legal profession tribute at the end of our days; in fact it never was.

With the end of an outmoded system now in sight, the probate attorneys and judges are not going away quietly. Their private retirement fund, long considered almost their birthright, is headed for the dumpster. Already they are working overtime to twist and mold its replacement, the living trust, so that the public will still be required to drop a portion of their life savings into the attorney's outstretched basket before departing to the hereafter. I am just as determined that such a tragedy not come to pass.

One last time I will point out to you that a living trust is first and foremost a concept of ownership and not some official-looking document from the computer of your attorney's secretary. I have said it a half-dozen times and will say it again: the first requirement is that you place your assets into the name of a controllable intermediary (your living trust) that will pay to you all the benefits from those assets while you are alive, and, after you are dead, pass the ownership of those assets on to the people you have chosen to receive them.

Beyond transferring your assets into the name of the trust and composing this simple contract, nothing else is legally required to form a living trust. Even such accompanying forms as the pour-over will, durable power of attorney, and the other auxiliary forms are not required appendages. Like Orville and Wilbur Wright's motorized kite at Kitty Hawk, the simplest of living trusts will fly with nothing but a skeleton structure.

Only you, the would-be grantor of a living trust, can supply the spark to ignite the plan. However, dealing with anything that brings us face-to-face with the prospect of dying is an unpleasant assignment that often mires our very best effort in procrastination. In spite of all the world's mighty cathedrals, and the words and music of assurance that effervesce from such fountains of sustenance, death remains the great unknown adventure that few of us are audacious enough to look forward to totally free of anxiety. Nonetheless, it is a part of our experience on this planet.

Most would agree, however, that what we can do for our families and loved ones must be done before we embark down that dark passage. No one has yet returned to clean up a few "last-minute details" that were too long dawdled on and temporized.

A gaggle of professionals and specialists await your passing. Collectively they have invested millions of dollars betting that you and thousands like you will continue to put off until "next week" those things that you will someday put off a week too long. What people could have done for themselves and their families at little or no cost before they died, the experts will be only too happy to do later on for a handsome fee. Best of all, they have arranged it so at that time, the law will be on their side. The family must sit impotently by while the professionals perform their voodoo in the stately building with the clock on top in the village square.

The law has provided you (probably by accident) with three different techniques of titling your private assets: sole ownership, joint tenancy and, what has been called by many, the finest gift that anyone can bequeath to their family: a revocable living trust.

Remember, no one can make it happen but you. You will leave one of two legacies: you will either continue down your present path and, in so doing, procrastinate your family right into probate court where they will pay the penalty for your inaction. Or you will forge a new path and transform destiny for both yourself and for your family.

The choice is yours.

# Appendix A

# Twenty-Five Popular Estate-Planning Myths

Many of the estate-planning myths that follow have actually originated in the offices of attorneys. Others are the result of the rumor mills that flourish in the barbershops, beauty parlors, and bowling alleys of America. Those originating with attorneys are designed purely to keep the unenlightened from consigning their affairs to a living trust—and in the market for a long and expensive ordeal in probate court.

### Myth #1: A living trust is a complex document that must be drawn by an attorney.
TRUTH: A living trust is not a document. It is a technique of titling assets, as are sole ownership, joint ownership, and corporations.

### Myth #2: Joint ownership of assets avoids probate.
TRUTH: Joint ownership of assets only delays probate. When the surviving owner dies the estate must then be probated.

### Myth #3: Estates of $600,000 or less do not require probate.

**TRUTH:** The $600,000 figure for years was the level at which estate taxes kicked in and had nothing to do with probate. The necessity of probate begins with the very first dollar in many states.

### Myth #4: A Last Will and Testament avoids probate.

**TRUTH:** All wills must be authenticated or proven in probate court. The word "probate" is a Latin term that means "to prove the will." Thus, a will is a mandatory summons to an expensive, twelve-to-twenty-four month long probate court procedure. If you have a will, your estate is headed for probate.

### Myth #5: A living trust is in reality a loophole in the tax law that will ultimately be closed by Congress.

**TRUTH:** Living trusts became a legal part of English Common Law nearly 500 years ago and are indirectly protected by the Tenth Amendment to the United States Constitution. The amendment leaves certain private rights to the states that include the right to do business as a corporation, under an assumed name, or form a trust. The outlawing of trusts would require an amendment to the United States Constitution and to the constitutions of all fifty states.

### Myth #6: Giving joint ownership of real estate to legal-age children avoids probate.

**TRUTH:** Joint ownership of real estate with such children sets the children up for eventual capital gains taxes that will usually exceed the cost of probating the estate. It will also risk the parents' assets in the case of a legal judgement against the children.

### Myth #7: A parent is free to sell real estate held jointly with adult children at any time.

**TRUTH:** Giving a child joint ownership in real estate makes the child a legal owner of the property and a sale of the property cannot be consummated without the child's willingness to sign off his share of the property.

## Myth #8: An attorney can write a clause into a will that will allow it to avoid probate.

**TRUTH:** Probate is a proving process from which no will is immune.

## Myth #9: Adding a clause to a will disinheriting any heir that challenges the terms of the will makes the will incontestable.

**TRUTH:** Such clauses (often referred to as "terror clauses") are installed in the will for the sole purpose of frightening the heir and have absolutely no merit in a court of law.

## Myth #10: Due to their complexity, living trusts are very expensive and take weeks to prepare.

**TRUTH:** Most living trust documents and auxiliary forms are completed by the attorney's secretary on a computer from commercially purchased software in less than an hour.

## Myth #11: Transferring assets to a living trust is complex and requires a trained professional.

**TRUTH:** Transferring assets to a trust is no more complicated than opening a checking account and usually requires less than fifteen minutes.

## Myth #12: You will lose control of your assets if you place them in a trust before your die.

**TRUTH:** You may designate yourself as the trustee (manager) of the trust and have complete control to do with the assets as you wish; sell them, spend them, buy more of them, trade them or give them away. Also, trustees and successor trustees must abide by the terms set in the living trust document.

## Myth #13: The trust grantor must apply to the Internal Revenue Service for an official trust number.

**TRUTH:** The social security number you have had for years is used to identify the trust. In fact there is no earthly reason why the IRS needs to know that you have a trust until after your death.

### Myth #14: A special income tax form must be filed every year by the trust.

**TRUTH:** The grantor of the trust is considered to be the primary beneficiary of the trust and entitled to all profits made by the trust. That income (or loss) is reported on the grantor's standard 1040 tax form just as if no trust existed.

### Myth #15: A living trust must be recorded with the local probate court.

**TRUTH:** Recording a trust with either probate court or the registrar of deeds office is poor practice. There is no need to do it and it turns a totally private contract into a public contract. Anyone can then request to see the private details of the trust.

### Myth #16: An attorney must determine the legality of a living trust.

**TRUTH:** The legality of a living trust is determined by the grantor's financial custodians (bank, stockbroker, or credit union). An attorney has absolutely nothing to say about the legality of a living trust.

### Myth #17: A living trust is not legal in any other state except the one in which it was written.

**TRUTH:** A living trust has no domicile and is legal in every state of the union and every free country of the world regardless of where it was written.

### Myth #18: A bank or trust company must be appointed as trustee of a living trust.

**TRUTH:** Professional trustees such as banks and trust companies are very expensive. Assets held in trust accounts are no more difficult to manage than assets held privately.

### Myth #19: All assets belonging to the trust must be listed in the trust contract.

**TRUTH:** Trust assets do not require listing in a living trust. Such a listing of assets serves only to add several pages to a trust contract for which an attorney can charge and in effect is a financial statement that gives a picture of what the client can afford.

**Myth #20: It takes six weeks or more to set up a living trust.**

**TRUTH:** If necessary, a living trust can usually be created (all documents drawn and all assets transferred to the trust) in three or four days.

**Myth #21: living trusts should be created after a person retires.**

**TRUTH:** To protect heirs properly, a trust should be created at the time a person begins to accumulate assets.

**Myth #22: A revocable living trust will protect a family from the nursing home costs of an elderly family member and also avoid lawsuits.**

**TRUTH:** Living trusts are designed to avoid the high costs and time of probate, and to minimize estate taxes. They do not reduce a family's obligation to pay nursing home costs or render a person judgment-proof.

**Myth #23: A trust grantor seriously risks being scammed if the trust is not drawn by an attorney.**

**TRUTH:** Because a trust is a technique of titling assets and not a document, no financial custodian will transfer assets from private to trust ownership unless satisfied that the trust contract is in order. For this reason there is no such thing as an illegal living trust. However, attorneys continue to frighten clients with this fable.

**Myth #24: A verbal will requires only witnesses and need not be a written document.**

**TRUTH:** Verbal wishes expressed by a person have absolutely no merit in probate court regardless of how many people have heard them.

**Myth #25: Assets transferred to a trust are physically owned by the trustee.**

**TRUTH:** Assets transferred to a trust are physically and legally owned by the trust and managed by the trustee.

# Appendix B

# Sample Documents of a Living Trust

There are many documents included in a well-prepared living trust. Most of them, such as the pour-over will, financial power of attorney, and health care power attorney, are supplementary. These and a handful of auxiliary forms cover a few minor gaps in a living trust. Your living trust can function without them but will probably not do the complete job you want it to do.

Presented here are samples of all the documents that should be present in your living trust package, completed for a fictional single person named John R. Perkins. Supplementary documents and auxiliary forms are very generic and vary little in text from one trust to the next. However, the Declaration of Trust is a different matter. There are many options that can be added to the Declaration of Trust to customize it to each individual's needs. It would require several hundred pages to print here every one of the possible combinations.

For example, you may want to name all of your children as co-successor trustees rather than naming just one as sole trustee. Should your estate be pushing the size level where you will be required to pay federal estate taxes, you may want to add the A-B living trust option that will in effect double your estate tax exemption. You may have underage or handicapped children and require a children's trust within your living trust to protect them from a probate court conservatorship. You may have decided that you would like to leave whole, undivided assets to your beneficiaries rather than leaving everything to them in shares. Or perhaps one of your beneficiaries has an outstanding loan with you, and you would like his indebtedness to be deducted from his inheritance. The possibilities go on and on.

For this reason, the Declaration of Trust presented in this series of sample documents is very basic and covers only the barest of essentials. Its purpose to give you a general idea of the makeup of a living trust contract. It may not fit your personal situation and you are urged to exercise caution in using it as a format to write your own trust contract.

# DECLARATION OF TRUST

Endeavoring to be legally bound, on this _____ day of _____,
20_____, I, John R. Perkins of 1234 Centerbrook Ave., Anywhere, California, referred to hereafter as the Grantor, acknowledge and proclaim that I hereby convey, transfer, assign and deliver to the
trustees of the hereby created revocable inter vivos TRUST all our right, title, and interest to certain
of our jointly and separately held assets.

This Trust shall be known as the John Perkins Trust and as the grantor of said Trust, I hereby
appoint John R. Perkins of Anywhere, California, hereafter known as the Trustee, to administer
those assets held in the above named Trust under the terms and conditions as set forth in this
Declaration of Trust.

In the occurrence of the resignation, incompetency or death of the surviving trustee, the grantor
hereby appoints in order listed:

Thomas B. Perkins, 567 Worthington St., Anywhere, California
Raymond J. Perkins, 891 Circle Avenue, Anywhere, California
Judith R. Posthumus, 321 N. 37th Street, Hometown, Colorado

Upon assuming the trusteeship the successor trustee shall be bound by the conditions and have all
the powers and authorities granted to trustee as set forth in this Trust and, upon assuming such
duties and authorities of the trusteeship, shall be recognized and acknowledged as trustee.

The grantor declares that the assets held in this Trust shall consist of properties which carry
verification of title evidencing them to be assets of this Trust, including but not limited to
assets registered by title approximating the ensuing form: "John R. Perkins, Trustee under date
of trust _____ ."

The grantor retains the right to remove assets from the Trust or add other assets to the Trust. The
aggregate of assets included in the Trust at any time shall be referred to as the Trust Estate.

CONDITIONS AND TERMS OF TRUST ADMINISTRATION: The grantor of the Trust hereby
conveys to the trustee(s) such discretionary powers necessary and appropriate to administer this
Trust, including but not limited to the power to sell, mortgage, encumber, pledge, hypothecate,
lease, rent, improve, repair, maintain, invest and reinvest the Trust Estate property. The trustee(s)
hereby accept(s) these powers and all other conditions and terms of this Declaration of Trust and
agree(s) to care for and manage the Trust Estate prudently with such actions as deemed in the best
interest and furtherance of the Trust.

After the payment of all taxes, assessments, and all charges incidental to the management of the Trust, the disposition of the principal and the net income generated by the Trust Estate shall be as follows:

During the lifetime of the grantor, the trustee(s) shall pay to the grantor as primary beneficiary of the Trust all income of the Trust Estate and such portions of the principal as the grantor from time to time directs, or otherwise as directed by the grantor during his/her life, or as it may appear necessary for the welfare, health, education, comfort and maintenance of the customary lifestyle of the grantor or his/her dependents during the physical or mental incompetence of the grantor.

Upon the death of the grantor, the trustee shall pay from the Trust Estate, if so directed by the personal representative of the grantor's estate, the funeral and burial expenses as well as any indebtedness of a final illness of the then deceased grantor. In the absence of any probate proceedings the trustee shall settle such claims from the Trust Estate. Upon the settlement of the current private, commercial and governmental obligations of the Trust and grantor, the trustee shall distribute the residue of the Trust Estate as directed in the Schedule of Trust Beneficiaries attached hereto and made a part of this document according to the terms and conditions of the Schedule of Trust Beneficiaries and all other sections, amendments and memorandums of and to this Trust.

## SCHEDULE OF TRUST BENEFICIARIES:

In the event of the disappearance of the grantor the trustee shall assume the administration and management of the Trust according to the provisions set forth in this Declaration of Trust. After a period of twelve (12) months, should the grantor not be heard from or body found, the Trust Estate shall be distributed to the beneficiaries as provided in the Schedule of Trust Beneficiaries.

After consideration of any outright distributions of undivided assets listed in this Schedule of Trust Beneficiaries, the balance of the Trust Estate shall be distributed, subject to amendments and memorandums to the trust, to the following first listed five (5) persons, in shares indicated:

Thomas B. Perkins - son
Raymond J. Perkins - son
Judith R. Posthumus - daughter
Carl K. Perkins - son
Margaret B. Grant - daughter

Upon this distribution should there be no remaining residue within the Trust Estate and the trustee(s) shall terminate the trust.

When a Children's Trust has not been included in the John Perkins Trust, trustees shall not be entitled to compensation for administering the Trust.

The physical or mental incapacity of the grantor shall be certified in writing by two physicians not related by blood or marriage to the grantor or any beneficiary of the hereby created Trust. Upon written confirmation of a return to physical or mental competency of a previously afflicted grantor by two physicians not related by blood or marriage to either of the grantors or to any beneficiary of the hereby created Trust, said grantor shall again assume the full responsibilities of grantor as set forth in the terms and conditions of this Declaration of Trust.

No interest of a beneficiary of this Trust can be alienated. No beneficiary can assign, pledge, encumber or otherwise transfer an interest in the Trust estate, nor shall such interest be garnished, attached, or levied upon or otherwise subjected to any proceedings whether at law or in equity.

Each beneficiary of the Trust hereby created shall be liable for his/her proportionate share of any estate taxes that may be imposed by any local, state or federal entity upon the share of the Trust Estate held for or distributed to a beneficiary upon the death of the grantor.

Upon the death of the grantor the decisions of successor trustee(s) shall be final and binding in regard to vague or unclear provisions of the Trust subject to dispute among the parties to the Trust.

The grantor hereby exempts this Declaration of Trust from the registration requirement of any municipality, court, government or public agency. Trustees shall be forbidden to disclose trust information to any municipality, court, government or public agency other than authorized government tax authorities.

This Trust shall be enforced, interpreted, and administered in accordance with the laws of the state of California.

Trustees shall serve without bond.

The grantor expressly reserves the right to alter, amend, modify or revoke any part of this Trust deemed revocable as created by this Declaration of Trust.

I execute this, the John Perkins Trust on _____ , 20_____ and certify that this Declaration of Trust correctly states the terms and conditions under which the trust property is to be held, managed and disposed of by the trustee(s).

(sig)_____

John R. Perkins, Grantor

The foregoing Declaration of Trust naming John R. Perkins as Grantor of the Trust is hereby approved and accepted.


(sig) _____

John R. Perkins, Trustee


State of _____

County of _____

On _____ , 20_____ the personally known to me grantor and trustee(s) of the John Perkins Trust created by this Declaration of Trust agreement, came before me and acknowledged that it was their free act and deed to execute this agreement.

_____

Notary Public
My commission expires: _____

Notary Seal:

# LAST WILL AND TESTAMENT OF JOHN R. PERKINS

I, John R. Perkins residing this date at 1234 Centerbrook Avenue, Anywhere, California, being of legal age and of sound and disposing mind and memory, do make, publish and declare this to be my Last Will and Testament, hereby revoking all wills and codicils by me heretofore made.

I am at this date single.

At my death I direct the following:

ONE:  I request that all of my just and enforceable debts and funeral expenses be paid out of my estate as soon as practicable after the time of my decease.

I further direct that all estate, inheritance, succession and other death taxes which shall become payable by reason of my death be paid out of my estate as an administrative expense.

TWO:  I give, devise and bequeath the residue of my entire estate, whether real property or personal property, of every kind, name, and description, whatsoever and wheresoever situated which I now own or hereafter acquire to John R. Perkins, Trustee, or the successor Trustees of the John Perkins Trust, to be held, managed and disposed of in accordance with the provisions of said Trust which was established by a Declaration of Trust dated _____ , 20_____ between John R. Perkins as the Grantor, and John R. Perkins as the Trustee, and which is now in existence.

THREE:  I appoint Thomas B. Perkins, 567 Worthington Street, Anywhere, California, to be my Personal Representative of this, my Last Will and Testament, hereby authorizing and empowering my said Personal Representative to compound, compromise, and settle and adjust all claims, demands and debts which may be presented against my estate or which may be due to my estate; and to sell at private or public sales, lease or exchange, at such prices and upon such terms of credit or otherwise as said Personal Representative may deem best, the whole or any part of my real or personal property; and to execute, acknowledge and deliver deeds or other proper instruments of conveyance thereof to the purchaser or purchasers, all without license or leave of court. I authorize my Personal Representative to employ real estate brokers to assist in the sale of any real estate and to pay such brokers standard commissions for their services.

In the event that the above named Personal Representative appointee shall be unable or unwilling to serve, I hereby appoint Raymond J. Perkins, 891 Circle Avenue, Anywhere, California as my alternate Personal Representative.

I request that no bond be required of my Personal Representative.

I subscribe my name to this Last Will and Testament this _____ day of _____, 20_____ at (city) _____ , (county) _____ , (state) _____

(sig) _____

John R. Perkins

On the date last written above, John R. Perkins declared to us, the undersigned witnesses, this instrument as his/her Last Will and Testament and requested us to act as witnesses to it. John R. Perkins thereupon signed this instrument in our presence, all of us being present at the same time. We now at his/her request and in his/her presence, and in the presence of each other, have signed this instrument as witnesses.

We declare under penalty of perjury that the foregoing is true and correct.

(sig)_____ , Witness

residing at (city) _____ , (county) _____ , (state) _____

(sig) _____ , Witness

residing at (city) _____ , (county) _____ , (state) _____

(sig) _____ , Witness

residing at (city) _____ , (county) _____ , (state) _____

# LIMITED FINANCIAL POWER OF ATTORNEY

## *(Durable)*

I, John R. Perkins, the principal, of 1234 Centerbrook Avenue, Anywhere, California, make this power of attorney according the laws of the state of California. I also revoke any prior power of attorney I may have made dealing with my financial affairs as described below.

1. APPOINTMENT OF AGENT.    I appoint Thomas B. Perkins, 567 Worthington Street, Anywhere, California, as my agent. If that person fails, for any reason, to serve as my agent, I appoint as successor agent Raymond J. Perkins, 891 Circle Avenue, Anywhere, California.

2. DURATION.    This power of attorney shall take effect when I sign it. The power of attorney shall not be affected by my disability.

3. POWERS OF AGENT.    The agent shall be limited to the power to convey, transfer, assign or deliver any real or personal property evidenced by right, title, or interest to be mine to John R. Perkins as Trustee of the John Perkins Trust, to be held, managed and disposed of in accordance with the provisions of said Trust which was established by a Declaration of Trust dated _____, 20_____ , between John R. Perkins as Grantor, and John R. Perkins as the Trustee and which is now in existence.

Such personal property shall include but not be limited to furniture, furnishings, antiques, art works, clothing, automobiles, recreational vehicles, tools, stocks, bonds, securities, mutual funds, certificates of deposit, dividends, drafts, checks, checking accounts, savings accounts, money market accounts, annuities, life insurance proceeds, retirement fund proceeds, gold, silver, diamonds, precious metals and stones, employment stock option plans, notes receivable and first and second trust deeds.

4. COMPENSATION OF AGENT.    The agent may receive reimbursement for actual and necessary expenses incurred in carrying out the powers conveyed by this instrument. Otherwise, the agent shall not receive any compensation.

5. RELIANCE BY THIRD PARTIES.    Third parties can rely on this power of attorney or the agent's representations about it. Anyone who does shall not be liable to me for permitting the agent to exercise powers under this power of attorney unless they have actual knowledge that this power of attorney has been terminated.

**6. MISCELLANEOUS.** This power of attorney shall be governed by California law, however it may be used out of state. Photocopies of this document carrying my original signature shall have the same legal authority as the original copy.

I am 18 years of age or older and of sound mind. I am signing this power of attorney voluntarily and without undue influence, duress or fraud.

I sign my name to this power of attorney on _____ , 20_____ .


(sig) _____
John R. Perkins, Principal

Witnesses:

_____

_____

State of _____
County of _____

This instrument was acknowledged before me on _____ , 20_____ by John R. Perkins.

Notary Public

_____ County, _____ State _____

My commission expires _____

Notary Seal:
Prepared by
John R. Perkins, 1234 Centerbrook Avenue, Anywhere, California

# HEALTH CARE POWER OF ATTORNEY

## *(Durable)*

I, John R. Perkins, the patient, of 1234 Centerbrook Avenue, Anywhere, California, execute this power of attorney according to the probate code of California on the _____ day of _____ , 20_____ . Execution of this instrument revokes any prior power of attorney I may have made concerning my health care.

1. DESIGNATION OF PATIENT ADVOCATE.   I designate Thomas B. Perkins, 567 Worthington Street, Anywhere, California, or Raymond J. Perkins, 891 Circle Avenue, Anywhere, California, as my patient advocate.

2. POWERS OF PATIENT ADVOCATE.   My patient advocate shall make all decisions in regard to my medical care, treatment and custody where permitted by law and not restricted by any other limitations of this power of attorney. My patient advocate is authorized to place me in or discharge me from hospitals, nursing homes, or any health care or recovery institution and shall have full authority to engage or dismiss physicians, nurses, therapists or any dispenser of health care and to reasonably compensate them from my funds and entitlements. Such patient advocate shall have access to all information concerning my state of health and to give medical waivers and authorize or refuse any medical, diagnostic, surgical, therapeutic, or convalescent procedure.

3. WAIVING OF LIFE-SUSTAINING TREATMENT. (optional)   By affixing below my signature upon this paragraph, I authorize the patient advocate with the power to withhold or withdraw treatment that would allow me to die at the patient advocate's discretion. I knowingly make this decision with the full cognizance that my death could ensue from such a judgment.

(sig) _____

John R. Perkins, Patient

4. EXERCISE OF POWERS.   Decisions of the patient advocate shall be made in accordance with my best interests unless otherwise directed in my handwriting below:
(List special conditions here)

5. DURATION.   This power of attorney shall take effect at such time as I am not able to join in medical treatment decisions concerning my health. The determination of my inability to take part in such decisions shall be made by my attending physician and another physician or licensed psychologist in writing. My disability shall not affect this power of attorney.

6. RELIANCE BY THIRD PARTIES.   Third parties can rely on this power of attorney, the doctors' statements or the patient advocate's representations about them. Anyone who does shall not be liable to me for permitting the patient advocate to exercise powers under the power of attorney, unless they have actual knowledge that this power of attorney has been revoked.

7. MISCELLANEOUS.   This power of attorney shall be governed by the laws of California, however it may be used out of state. Originally signed photocopies of this document shall have the same legal authority as the original document.

Being of sound mind and of the age of 18 or older I sign my name to this instrument on _____ , 20_____ free of undue influence, duress, or fraud.


(sig) _____

John R. Perkins, Patient

### STATEMENT OF WITNESSES

We consider ourselves eligible to serve as witnesses and have witnessed the patient's signature, and state that the patient appears to be of sound mind and under no undue influence, duress, or fraud.


_____

Signature of Witness

_____

Print Name of Witness

_____

Street Address of Witness

City _____ State _____ Zip _____


_____

Signature of Witness

_____

Print Name of Witness

_____

Street Address of Witness

City _____ State _____ Zip _____

_____

Signature of Witness

_____

Print Name of Witness

_____

Street Address of Witness

City _____ State _____ Zip _____

## ACCEPTANCE OF DESIGNATION

I have been designated as the patient advocate of the patient making this power of attorney. I accept that designation and agree to act as required by law and as stated below:

(a) This designation shall not become effective unless the patient is unable to participate in medical treatment decisions.

(b) A patient advocate shall not exercise powers concerning the patient's care, custody, and medical treatment that the patient, if the patient were able to participate in the decision, could not have exercised on his own behalf.

(c) This designation cannot be used to make a medical treatment decision to withhold or withdraw treatment from a patient who is pregnant that would result in the pregnant patient's death.

(d) A patient advocate may make a decision to withhold or withdraw treatment which would allow a patient to die only if the patient has expressed in a clear and convincing manner that the patient advocate is authorized to make such a decision, and that the patient acknowledges that such a decision could or would result in the patient's death.

(e) A patient advocate shall not receive compensation for the performance of his/her authority, rights, and responsibilities, but a patient advocate may be reimbursed for actual and necessary expenses incurred in the performance of his or her authority, rights and responsibilities.

(f) A patient advocate shall act in accordance with the standards of care applicable to fiduciaries when acting for the patient and shall act consistent with the patient's best interests. The known desires of the patient expressed or evidenced while the patient is able to participate in medical treatment decisions are presumed to be in the patient's best interests.

(g) A patient may revoke his/her designation at any time and in any manner sufficient to communicate an intent to revoke.

(h) A patient advocate may revoke his/her acceptance to the designation at any time and in any manner sufficient to communicate an intent to revoke.

(i) A patient admitted to a health facility or agency has the rights enumerated in the Public Health Code of the state of California.

Date _____

(sig) _____

Acting Patient Advocate

## DOCTORS' STATEMENT

I, _____ of _____ am the patient's attending physician.

I, _____ of _____ am either a physician or licensed psychologist.

We have examined the patient and it is our opinion that the patient is unable to participate in medical treatment decisions.

_____        _____
Date                                          Attending Physician

_____        _____
Date                                          Attending Physician

# AFFIDAVIT OF TRUST EXISTENCE

Be it acknowledged, that I, John R. Perkins of 1234 Centerbrook Avenue, Anywhere, California 89333, the undersigned deponents being of legal age, do declare and say under oath as grantor that an inter vivos trust referred to as the John Perkins Trust exists as of _____ .
date of trust execution
The grantor also declares that John R. Perkins has been appointed to serve as trustee of the aforesaid John Perkins Trust with full powers to administer those assets held in the above named Trust under the terms and conditions as set forth in that Declaration of Trust administering the John Perkins Trust.

Also, the grantor has appointed:

Thomas B. Perkins, 567 Worthington Street, Anywhere, California
Raymond J. Perkins, 891 Circle Avenue, Anywhere, California
Judith R. Posthumus, 321 N. 37th Street, Hometown, Colorado

as successor trustees to assume the administration of the trust upon the deaths of all primary trustees.

I further affirm that the foregoing is true except as to statements made upon information and belief, and as to those I believe them to be true.

Witness my hand under the penalties of perjury this date _____
date of trust execution


(sig) _____

John R. Perkins
1234 Centerbrook Avenue, Anywhere, California

STATE OF _____
COUNTY OF _____
On _____ before me, _____ , personally appeared John
date of trust execution        name of notary public
R. Perkins, personally known to me (or proved to me on the basis of satisfactory evidence) to be the person whose name is subscribed to the within instrument and acknowledged to me that he/she executed the same in his/her authorized capacities, and that by his/her signature on the instrument the person, or entity upon behalf of which the person acted, executed the instrument.

(Notary sig) _____ _____
Expiration of commission _____
Seal:   Affiant ___ known ___ unknown
ID Produced _____

# MEMORANDUM TO
# THE JOHN PERKINS TRUST

Memorandum No. _____

### DISTRIBUTION OF PERSONAL EFFECTS AND SPECIAL ASSETS

The trust grantor desires that upon his/her death certain assets and possessions shall be given to those hereafter indicated:

Description of
asset _____*Van Gogh painting*_____ Beneficiary _____*Thomas B. Perkins*_____

Description of
asset _____*Tool Collection*_____ Beneficiary _____*Raymond J. Perkins*_____

Description of
asset _____*Diamond Engagement Ring*_____ Beneficiary _____*Margaret B. Grant*_____

Description of
asset _____*Collection of Books in Residence*_____ Beneficiary _____*Carl K. Perkins*_____

Description of
asset _____ Beneficiary _____

Description of
asset _____ Beneficiary _____

Description of
asset _____ Beneficiary _____

Description of
asset _____ Beneficiary _____

Description of
asset _____ Beneficiary _____

Description of
asset _____ Beneficiary _____

No other personal effects or special assets are distributed by this memorandum.

Dated _____

(sig) _____
John R. Perkins, Grantor

# AMENDMENT TO THE JOHN PERKINS TRUST

This amendment to the John Perkins Trust shall be know as Amendment No. _____ and is made this _____ day of _____ , 20_____ by John R. Perkins, the grantor of the trust. Under the power of amendment reserved to the grantor by said trust, the grantor amends the trust as follows:

1. The following is added to the trust:

Carl K. Perkins is added as successor trustee.

No further additions to the trust are made with this amendment.

2. The following is deleted from the trust:

Thomas B. Perkins is deleted as successor trustee.

No further deletions from the trust are made with this amendment.

In all other respects, the trust as executed on _____ , 20_____ by the grantor is hereby affirmed.

(sig) _____

John R. Perkins, Grantor

The foregoing amendment to the instrument creating an inter vivos Trust dated _____ , 20 _____ listing John R. Perkins as grantor and known as the John Perkins Trust is hereby accepted and acknowledged.

(sig) _____

John R. Perkins, Trustee

County of _____

City of _____

State of _____

On _____ , 20 _____ the Grantor and Trustee of the trust estate created by the said inter vivos Trust and personally known to me came before me and acknowledged that it was their free act and deed to execute this amendment to the John Perkins Trust.

_____

Notary Public

My commission expires: _____

Notary Seal:

# BILL OF SALE
# OF TANGIBLE PERSONAL PROPERTY

I, John R. Perkins, hereinafter called the Grantor, do give, grant, bargain, sell and convey to the Trustees of the trust known as the John Perkins Trust, all right, title and interest in and to the following tangible personal property:

All tangible personal property normally kept at the residences of the Grantor listed the following addresses:

Residence, 1234 Centerbrook Avenue, Anywhere, California
Cottage, 3456 Tahoe Rapids, Small Town, Nevada

Such tangible personal property shall include, but not be limited to, furniture, furnishings, dishes and china, tableware, sporting goods, trailers, boats, guns, books, paintings, other art objects, jewelry, collections of personal property, lawn furniture, tools, machinery and maintenance equipment, and items attached to the residence but not considered real estate; all insurance policies on said tangible personal property and the proceeds from said policies resulting from claims therefrom and the following additional personal property:

The Grantor warrants that all said tangible personal property is owned by the Grantor free and clear of all claims or liens and all said tangible personal property can be transferred by the Grantor.

Dated: _____

(sig) _____

John R. Perkins,
Grantor and Trustee

# QUITCLAIM DEED

This Quitclaim Deed, executed on this date of _____ by the first party (the grantors):

John R. Perkins, 1234 Centerbrook Avenue, Anywhere, California,

in favor of the second party (the grantee):

The John Perkins Trust, John R. Perkins, Trustee, 1234 Centerbrook Avenue, Anywhere, California

Witness that the said first party, for good consideration and for the sum of less than one hundred dollars paid by the said second party, the receipt whereof is hereby acknowledged, does hereby forever remise, release and quitclaim to the said second party all the right, title, interest and claim which the said first party has in and to the following parcel of land, and improvements and appurtenances thereto to the County of Treetop, State of California to wit:

Lots 2 & 3 of the Herman addition to Anywhere, Treetop County, California

In witness whereof, the said first party has signed and sealed these presents the day and year first above written, signed, sealed and delivered in presence of the following grantors:

X _____
John R. Perkins, 1234 Centerbrook Avenue, Anywhere, California

Witness signature _____

Print name _____

Witness signature _____

Print name _____

State of _____
County of _____

On this date _____ the grantor(s) of this Quitclaim Deed personally known to me appeared before me (or proved to me on the basis of satisfactory evidence) to be the person(s) whose name(s) is/are subscribed in this instrument and acknowledged to me that he/she/they executed the same in his/her/their authorized capacity(ies) and that by his/her/their signatures(s) on the instrument the person(s), or the entity upon witness my hand and official seal.

_____

Signature of Notary

My commission expires _____

Affiant _____ Known _____ Produced ID
Type of ID _____

Prepared by:
John R. Perkins
1234 Centerbrook Avenue, Anywhere, California

_____

Signature

# IRREVOCABLE STOCK OR BOND POWER FORM

For value received, the undersigned does/do hereby sell, assign and transfer to:

Taxpayer I.D. number or Social Security Number

IF STOCK, COMPLETE THIS PORTION

_____ shares of the _____ stock of _____
represented by Certificate(s) Numbers(s) _____ inclusive, standing
the name of the undersigned on the books of said Company.

IF BONDS, COMPLETE THIS PORTION

_____ bonds of _____ in the
principal amount of $ _____ number(s) _____ inclusive,
standing in the name of the undersigned on the books of said Company.

The undersigned does/do hereby irrevocably constitute and appoint _____
Attorney to transfer the said stock or bond(s), as the case may be, on the books of said Company,
with Full power of substitution in the premises.

Dated _____

X _____

X _____
Signature of person(s) executing this power

# ASSIGNMENT

Know all men by these presents that I, John R. Perkins, the individual named as the owner and holder of a certain Land Contract from Douglas and Donna Dickens to me and recorded in the Land Records of Treetop County, state of California in Vol. _____ , Page _____ do hereby assign transfer and set over unto John R. Perkins, or his successor, as trustee under the terms of a certain inter vivos trust dated _____ and known as the John Perkins Trust all of my right, title and interest in and to said contract and to the note or other evidence of indebtedness intended to be secured by such contract.

[Legal description of property]

Lot 4 of the Herman addition to Anywhere, Treetop County, California

To have and to hold as such trustees forever, and I declare that neither I nor my heirs or assigns shall have or make any claim or demand pursuant to such instrument.

In witness whereof, I have hereunto set my hand and seal this _____ day of _____ , 20_____ .

(sig) _____

John R. Perkins, assignor

Signed and acknowledged in the presence of:

(sig) _____ , Witness

Print name _____

(sig) _____ , Witness

Print name _____

State of California, County of _____

City, village, township of _____

On the _____ day of _____ , 20_____ personally appeared John R. Perkins, known to me to be the individual who executed the foregoing instrument and acknowledged the same to be his free act and deed before me.

(sig) _____ Notary Public

Print name _____

My commission expires _____

Notary Seal:

# Glossary

**A-B living trust**

A common trust that upon the death of the first spouse converts to two sub-trusts, entitled Trust A and Trust B. An A-B living trust enables a married couple to use both of its estate tax exemptions, in effect doubling the amount of its estate tax exemption

**agent**

In estate planning, a person that has been given power of attorney to handle financial matters for you

**assignment form**

In estate planning, assigns the credit from money due to you personally by a debtor (such as a person that has purchased property from you on a land contract) to your living trust

**attorney-in-fact**

Sometimes referred to as an agent, a person who has been granted power of attorney to act for you in financial matters

**bill of sale**

In estate planning, transfers untitled property owned personally by you to the ownership of your living trust

**capital gains tax**

Taxation on profits from the sale of assets due to their appreciation during ownership

### charitable remainder trust

An irrevocable trust in which an IRS-approved charity serves as trustee and manages or invests property in the trust; a portion of the income from the property goes to the trust grantor for a specified payment period, after which the property is donated to the charity

### children's trust

A sub-trust within the original trust contract that instructs the successor trustee to distribute the principal of the trust to children at or over a predetermined legal gage in a lump sum or over several payments

### conservator

A court-appointed person legally set in charge of all financial matters of a minor or person legally judged to be mentally incompetent (also known as a *property guardian*)

### contingent beneficiaries

Those persons that will receive the assets and benefits of the trust after the grantor of the trust is dead

### durable financial power of attorney

A document that gives an agent power to act in financial matters for another person even if that person has been judged incompetent

### estate

Also known as "net estate," the value of the total possessions (assets) owned by a living or deceased person minus the total obligations owed. "Gross estate" refers to the value of the total assets owned by a living or deceased person *without* deducting the obligations owed

### estate tax

A tax imposed by the federal government and sometimes a state government on the excess in an estate after a statute exemption has been applied

### executor

The personal representative appointed by a decedent before death that will intercede for the decedent's wishes during the probating of the estate

**financial custodians**

Banks, stockbrokers, insurance companies, credit unions, and similar institutions that hold an individual's assets in safekeeping

**generation-skipping tax**

A federal tax sometimes imposed when the assets of a decedent bypass the next generation and go instead to the following generation (grandchildren)

**grantor**

The person(s) that transfers assets from private ownership to trust ownership, thereby creating a trust (sometimes known as a "trustor" or "settlor")

**health care power of attorney**

Legally allows health care decisions to be made for a patient by an appointed advocate should the patient become physically or mentally incapable of making such decisions for himself

**heirs**

Those people, usually relatives of the deceased, considered most likely to inherit the assets of an estate. *Legal heirs* are those people, related or non-related, who according to a will or trust are to inherit part or all of an estate.

**holographic will**

A will written in the actual longhand script of the person making the will (as opposed to a will in which the text has been typed)

**intestate**

having made no legal or binding Last Will and Testament before death

**irrevocable trust**

a trust which, once made, cannot be canceled or altered by anyone, including its creator

**Joint Tenancy with Right of Survivorship**

a type of joint ownership in which two or more people share ownership of an asset, with the name of each joint owner appearing on the asset's title or deed

### Last Will and Testament

A written or typed statement that declares a person's intent of asset distribution at his death

### liquid assets

assets that are quickly converted to cash such as stocks, bonds, mutual funds, and certificates of deposit

### living trust

officially called a "revocable *inter vivos* trust," it is a technique of titling deeds and assets in the name of a fictitious entity, which holds ownership of those assets and, after the death of the grantor (maker of trust), distributes those assets according to the wishes of the grantor

### living will

grants a health care provider, such as a hospital or doctor, the legal authority to make health care decisions for you—including the right to make life-sustaining decisions

### payment-on-death beneficiary (P.O.D.)

designates on the title of the asset who will inherit that asset upon the death of the owner

### personal guardian

A person appointed to physically rear the children of a decedent; also one appointed to watch over the physical being of one judged to be physically or mentally incapacitated

### personal representative

see *executor*

### pour-over will

an auxiliary document that catches those inadvertent asset oversights that would otherwise have to undergo an intestate probate procedure

### power of attorney

a legal document that allows one person to act for another person

### primary beneficiaries

the grantors or makers of a revocable living trust who by law are entitled to all income and profit from the trust while alive

**probate**

a legal procedure of the state that guarantees the authenticity of a Last Will and Testament

**property guardian**

See *conservator*

**Qualified Terminal Property Trust**

commonly referred to as a "Q-Tip Trust" or an "A-B-C Trust." A married couple's net assets are split and placed equally in Trusts A and B, while assets exceeding the current exemption are placed in a Trust C. The total payment of any estate taxes on Trust C is deferred until after the death of the second spouse.

**revocable trust**

a trust in which the maker of the trust (grantor) has the right to change any detail of the trust contract at any time, including terminating the trust.

**successor trustee**

the person or firm that takes over family financial affairs upon the incapacity or death of the original trustees

**tenancy by the entirety**

a type of joint ownership that must involve a husband and wife and which can be terminated only by the mutual consent and joint action of both spouses during their lifetimes

**testate**

having drawn a legal and binding last Will and Testament before death

**trust company**

a commercial firm (often a division of a bank) acting as trustee that professionally manages and administers the affairs of trust

**trustee**

a manager or caretaker appointed by a trust's grantor to administer the affairs of the trust

# Directory of Tax Office Web Sites

It's sometimes difficult to keep up with federal and state tax laws. The following Web sites contain tax law updates and useful contact information.

**Federal:**   **United States Department of the Treasury** • http://www.ustreas.gov/
**Internal Revenue Service** • http://www.irs.gov/

**State:**   **Alabama**
Department of Revenue • http://www.ador.state.al.us

**Alaska**
Department of Revenue • http://www.revenue.state.ak.us

**Arizona**
Department of Revenue • http://www.revenue.state.az.us

**Arkansas**
Department of Finance & Administration • http://www.state.ar.us/dfa

**California**
Franchise Tax Board • http://www.taxes.ca.gov

**Colorado**
Department of Revenue • http://www.revenue.state.co.us

**Connecticut**
Department of Revenue Services • http://www.drs.state.ct.us

**Delaware**
Department of Finance Division of Revenue • http://www.state.de.us/revenue

**District of Columbia**
Office of Tax & Revenue • http://cfo.dc.gov/etsc/main.shtm

**Florida**
Department of Revenue • http://www.myflorida.com/dor

**Georgia**
Department of Revenue • http://www2.state.ga.us/Departments/DOR

**Hawaii**
Department of Taxation • http://www.state.hi.us/tax/tax.html

**Idaho**
State Tax Commission • http://www2.state.id.us/tax/index.html

**Illinois**
Department of Revenue • http://www.revenue.state.il.us

**Indiana**
Department of Revenue • http://www.in.gov/dor

**Iowa**

Department of Revenue • http://www.state.ia.us/tax

**Kansas**

Department of Revenue • http://www.ksrevenue.org

**Kentucky**

Revenue Cabinet • http://revenue.state.ky.us

**Louisiana**

Department of Revenue • http://www.rev.state.la.us

**Maine**

Revenue Services • http://www.state.me.us/revenue/homepage.html

**Maryland**

Comptroller of Maryland • http://www.comp.state.md.us

**Massachusetts**

Department of Revenue • http://www.massdor.com

**Michigan**

Department of Treasury • http://www.michigan.gov/treasury

**Minnesota**

Department of Revenue • http://www.taxes.state.mn.us

**Mississippi**

State Tax Commission • http://www.mstc.state.ms.us

**Missouri**

Department of Revenue Division of Taxation • http://www.dor.state.mo.us/tax

**Montana**

Department of Revenue • http://www.state.mt.us/revenue/css/default.asp

**Nebraska**

Department of Revenue • http://www.revenue.state.ne.us

**Nevada**

Department of Taxation • http://tax.state.nv.us

**New Hampshire**

Department of Revenue Administration • http://www.state.nh.us/revenue

**New Jersey**

Division of Taxation • http://www.state.nj.us/treasury/taxation

**New Mexico**

Taxation & Revenue Department • http://www.state.nm.us/tax

**New York**

Department of Taxation & Finance • http://www.tax.state.ny.us

**North Carolina**
Department of Revenue • http://www.dor.state.nc.us

**North Dakota**
Office of State Tax Commissioner • http://www.state.nd.us/taxdpt

**Ohio**
Department of Taxation • http://www.state.oh.us/tax

**Oklahoma**
Tax Commission • http://www.oktax.state.ok.us/

**Oregon**
Department of Revenue • http://www.dor.state.or.us

**Pennsylvania**
Department of Revenue • http://www.revenue.state.pa.us

**Rhode Island**
Division of Taxation • http://www.tax.state.ri.us

**South Carolina**
Department of Revenue • http://www.sctax.org

**South Dakota**
Department of Revenue • http://www.state.sd.us/revenue/revenue.html

**Tennessee**
Department of Revenue and Regulation • http://www.state.tn.us/revenue

**Texas**
Comptroller of Public Accounts • http://www.window.state.tx.us

**Utah**
State Tax Commission • http://tax.utah.gov

**Vermont**
Department of Taxes • http://www.state.vt.us/tax

**Virginia**
Department of Taxation • http://www.tax.state.va.us

**Washington**
Department of Revenue • http://dor.wa.gov

**West Virginia**
Department of Tax & Revenue • http://www.state.wv.us/taxrev

**Wisconsin**
Department of Revenue • http://www.dor.state.wi.us/

**Wyoming**
Department of Revenue • http://revenue.state.wy.us

# Index

Page numbers followed by *t* and *f* refer to tables and figures respectively.